MAKING UP ACCOUNTANTS

T0358412

Making Up Accountants

The organizational and professional socialization of trainee chartered accountants

FIONA ANDERSON-GOUGH
UMIST

CHRISTOPHER GREY
University of Leeds

KEITH ROBSON
UMIST

Routledge
Taylor & Francis Group

LONDON AND NEW YORK

First published 1998 by Ashgate Publishing

Reissued 2018 by Routledge
2 Park Square, Milton Park, Abingdon, Oxon, OX14 4RN
711 Third Avenue, New York, NY I 0017, USA

Routledge is an imprint of the Taylor & Francis Group, an informa business

Notice:
Product or corporate names may be trademarks or registered trademarks, and are used only for identification and explanation without intent to infringe.

Publisher's Note
The publisher has gone to great lengths to ensure the quality of this reprint but points out that some imperfections in the original copies may be apparent.

Disclaimer
The publisher has made every effort to trace copyright holders and welcomes correspondence from those they have been unable to contact.

A Library of Congress record exists under LC control number: 98071969

ISBN 13: 978-1-138-32749-8 (hbk)
ISBN 13: 978-0-429-44921-5 (ebk)

Contents

Acknowledgements

We gratefully acknowledge the financial support of the Research Board of the ICAEW and of our host institutions. We also acknowledge the excellent access and assistance offered by the two Big Six firms who took part in the study and the many individuals in both firms who gave generously of their time thus enabling the successful completion of the research.

1 Professional Socialization in Chartered Accountancy Practices

Introduction

The recruitment, training and socialization processes of professional associations, firms and partnerships have received considerable attention in the literature on, for example, the legal (e.g. Rueschemeyer, 1973; 1986; Abbott, 1988) and medical professions (e.g. Freidson, 1970; 1986). Socialization processes should *not* be confused with 'socializing' in its everyday sense of informal leisure-time friendships (cf. *Accountancy Age*, 14th March 1996). Whilst these latter may have a role in professional socialization, the term refers to the whole gamut of ways in which the meaning and conduct of professional membership is transmitted. This 'making' of professionals has been regarded as a crucial contributor to the success of the professionalization projects of particular occupations (see the readings in Dingwall and Lewis [eds], 1983). *Self-regulation* has been considered one of the essential traits of a professional organization, alongside the presence of an abstract body of knowledge, monopoly control of certain work tasks and a public service ethic: (cf. Goode, 1957; Greenwood, 1957; Parsons, 1968). The notion of self-regulation, however, can be considered not merely in terms of the bureaucratic authorities, rules, regulations and standards that govern work content and best practice in each profession (in accountancy, for example, the ethical guidelines and Disciplinary Committees, Members Handbooks, Accounting and Auditing Standards), but also in relation to the manner in which professionals conduct themselves with respect to other professionals and to the clients whom they service. Part of being a professional person involves a *'regulation of the self'* in terms of the articulation of a professional discourse, the following of formal and informal norms of conduct: in short, the expectation of appropriate personal and social behaviour from oneself and from others.

In this book we examine how this second type of self-regulatory norms is constructed for and communicated to trainee Chartered Accountants (CAs) in two of the large international ('Big Six') firms. The Big Six are those firms which dominate the markets for accounting and auditing services world-wide. Although it has been argued, and we would concur, that the process of socialization in professional firms is crucial to the professionalization projects of all professional occupations, and has been recognised as such in relation to many professions, there has been remarkably little study of the recruitment, training and socialization of accountants (see Harper, 1988; Power, 1991; Coffey, 1993; Dirsmith *et al*, 1997; Grey, 1994; 1998; Coffey, 1994; Hanlon, 1994 for the principal, albeit partial, exceptions). The research problematic with which we began was to examine how professional socialization occurs within the Big Six firms and how CA trainees within the firms identify with the concept of the profession and the professional. In the next section we elaborate our research problematic and outline the themes of the book.

1. Professional Socialization in CA Practices: Making Up Accountants

To qualify as a chartered accountant licensed by the Institute of Chartered Accountants in England and Wales (ICAEW) there are two formal requirements. First, it is necessary for trainees to pass the examinations set by the ICAEW, and, second, to prove to the ICAEW that they have undertaken the type and amount of work as set out by the ICAEW as a minimum standard of experience. To this end, the vast majority of people wishing to qualify as a CA apply for a training contract with an accounting firm that is authorised by the ICAEW. The training contract is usually for three years during which time the trainee agrees to work for the firm, and the firm agrees to provide the necessary work experience, examination tuition and to pay the examination fees. In recent years it has been the norm for those entering training contracts to be graduates.

The entry of new recruits into a profession has a number of common themes across different professions. Recruits receive specific training through formal (and costly) instruction: perhaps by correspondence course, through an organization of professional tutors or an institute of higher education. The explicit testing of instructed knowledge pertaining to professional or legal rules and regulations, abstractions from specific work practices and detail of technical procedures is one of the most obvious ways in which the profession can erect an effective barrier between the *professional*, who, having succeeded in completing his or her studies, is able to practice as an accountant, lawyer, etc., and the *layperson*, who is disallowed from such occupational tasks (Johnson, 1972; 1977; Willmott, 1986).

We contend, however, that the making of the professional accountant (or lawyer or clinician) is not reducible to the procedures for schooling and examining new entrants in the rules, regulations and procedures of the occupation. This assertion is borne out by the recognition that many professional groupings require prospective entrants to the profession to undertake a minimum period of training in practice - in the case of the ICAEW this means, with some recent exceptions, a period of training within public practice.

Although the period of public practice might be seen simply as a form of apprenticeship into the craft of accountancy and auditing, the attention to performing technical services to clients is only part of the experience and practice of becoming the professional person. The training of the auditor is also in large part a socialization into the organizational culture and professional norms of the employing firm. At the very outset, the recruitment of trainees is itself a social process in that interviewers and personnel staff examine the profiles and responses of applicants in interview in accordance with their conceptions of the 'professional' auditor, as well as the firm's 'type'. The training of new entrants to the profession embraces more than simply an inculcation into technical accounting and auditing procedures (and the examination techniques through which they are tested): the culture of the audit firm provides a new environment to which they must adapt themselves and identify what it means to be 'professional'. The focus of this book is upon the ways in which such an identity is acquired in the context of the informal, organizational norms of the firms studied. What organizational norms operate, how they are constructed and transformed, and how successfully trainee auditors recognise and accommodate themselves to those norms are key elements that structure, we would argue, the career path of trainee accountants: organizational socialization is thus an important component of the 'making' of professional accountants.

Earlier work has suggested that the nature of the formal and informal rules that structure professional success is complex (e.g. Becker *et al*, 1961). In the case of accounting this is in part the outcome of the training process that is first and foremost a commitment to an individual firm, competing with other firms, and not primarily a commitment to a professional grouping. As Abbott has noted with reference to the accountancy profession in the US, in such contexts 'the association of work with profession is broken, and with it much of the professional association's power' (Abbott, 1988, p.154). Such an observation illuminates some of the professional associations' difficulties in securing the consent of their membership to proposals for regulatory and structural change (Tricker, 1983; Worsley, 1985). As one influential senior professional has remarked:

"It seems that major internal reforms are only possible if the membership does not appreciate the significance of what is happening" (Davison, 1987, p.2).

Socialization in the auditing firm may, in addition, be complicated by the different organizational cultures present in each of the Big Six firms: we sought also to assess this claim.

Not only does professional socialization occur within firm-specific contexts but also within the added complexity of the general array of functions and services that the multi-national auditing firms now perform (Hopwood *et al*, 1989). The nature of the accountancy profession has become more complex as ever more diverse functions are performed by auditing firms: it is misleading to think of chartered accountancy as a homogenous profession (Robson and Cooper, 1990). Instead, and in common with some other professions, accounting firms are increasingly characterised by an assortment of functional and organizational pressures and loyalties that cut across the profession as a whole (Robson *et al*, 1994). We aimed to examine the extent to which the various tasks performed within the modern international auditing firm, some of which have no direct connection to the formal knowledge and training of auditors, may impact upon professional socialization, and vice versa.

2. Research Themes and Objectives

The research upon which this book is based used interview-based case studies to examine the processes through which audit trainees recognise, define and acquire the attributes of the accounting professional, and how those who are 'successful' in this are distinguished through the organizational culture from those who are not. The case studies were conducted in the regional offices of two major international accountancy firms.

2.1 Professional Socialization: Three Theses

The research focused upon three major issues:

* **What processes of socialization occur in the course of auditor training contracts, e.g. professional examination training, staff assessments and informal norm-setting?**

Thesis 1*: Socialization processes focus not only upon examination performance, but presentation to clients and ability to integrate with the social norms of peers, managers and partners.*

- **To what extent can the processes of professional and organizational socialization be separated, and to what extent do corporate culture initiatives within particular firms mitigate against, or contribute to, the maintenance of a coherent professional identity?**

Thesis 2*: The socialization of trainees is into organizational culture first and professional culture second.*

- **What is the impact of the functional divisions (e.g. audit, tax, insolvency) upon professional socialization?**

Thesis 3*: Socialization processes vary between divisions and give rise to differing conceptions of the role of the professional accountant.*

2.2 Research Methodologies and Methods

The research methods employed included semi-structured interviews and analysis of documentary evidence. Members of the personnel staff, training partners, seniors and trainees were interviewed by one or two of the researchers in a semi-structured format in order to elicit their views on and interpretations of the culture of their audit firm with respect to both formal and informal norms of 'professional' attitudes, behaviour and conduct. The interviews allowed the researchers to report and gain insight into the experiences and problems organizational actors face in recognising and following forms of approved 'professional' behaviour. Our methodological approach in this study owes its basis to ethnographic or, more broadly, phenomenological research in that rather than imposing meanings upon our research subjects we were concerned to explore the meanings that subjects gained and the processes through which they gained them during their socialization into the culture of their auditing firm. The research sought to *interpret* the understandings, as re-presented to us, that audit trainees acquired during their training contract on the issues of professional identity, firm identity, (and, indeed to what extent these concepts can be understood separately, if at all, by trainees), and the relationships of trainees to their professional institute.

Each interview lasted for approximately one hour and was tape recorded (when acceptable to the subject). The interviews with trainees were transcribed and analysed with the assistance of *The Ethnograph*, a Qualitative Data Analysis Software package. The research also examined the various forms of documentation on the appraisal of trainee auditors to inform the understanding of the construction of the professional accountant and his/her social world. The rules and regulations of the accountancy bodies pertaining to the training and examination process, and the manner in which these rules are translated within the professional firms were also studied in order to examine the influence of the wider project of professionalization that accountants have mobilised to enhance and to further their professional status.

In order to capture some variations in organizational culture across audit firms, two regional offices within two international ('Big Six') firms were selected as research sites. We were fortunate to secure excellent access to these firms which we refer to as Firm A and Firm B. We elaborate these methodological points in *Chapter 3*. The findings of our research are reported in *Chapter 4* (Thesis 1), *Chapter 5* (Thesis 2) and *Chapter 6* (Thesis 3).

2 Theories of Professions and Professional Socialization

Introduction

In this chapter we seek to address three issues. First, what are the main features or characteristics that 'professionals' themselves would stress in order to distinguish themselves as professionals to others? What is, or might be, the self-image of a profession? The question as to how trainee accountants are socialized as 'professionals' commonly presupposes that there are certain features in a discourse that we can identify as constituting professionalism: the professional discourse that contributes to the practices of being a 'professional'. Put another way, there might be ways of thinking about being professional that academics or, indeed, lay people would regard as differentiating a professional person from, say, a highly skilled car mechanic. Therefore one starting point for an analysis of professional socialization is an outline of the professional discourse as it is commonly or conventionally articulated.

The second issue we address in this chapter is how the organization and structure of accounting practices in the UK mediates the concept of being an accountant. Here we are concerned with the way in which the institutional and organizational arrangement of accounting practices may influence the idea of an identification with or affiliation to a profession. The form of professional identity assumed by accountants and auditors cannot be understood in the absence of an appreciation of the organization and structure of accounting practices in the UK and the tensions that emerge from these practices. We examine the professional context of accountancy and how the 'discourse' of the profession is enabled or constrained by the occupational arrangement and activities of accountants. In this way it is possible to consider what tensions have emerged for accountancy's 'professionalization project': the continuing process of maintaining a discourse that projects accountancy as a profession to its members and to important external agents. The examination of such an issue, however, is both speculative and preliminary to the analysis of our research into two Big Six firms and the views of trainees as to their identification with a profession. In the next

7

section we consider some of the conventional meanings attached to the notion of profession and being professional.

In the third part of this chapter we link our research to the existing research on professions more broadly. The main theoretical approaches to the study of the professions are outlined and the linkages between the three theses that we outlined in Chapter 1 and the theories of professions are established. We also review the existing research into the socialization of accountants and auditors.

1. Accountancy in the UK

As we will examine in detail in the next section of this chapter, conventional understandings of the term profession have tended to assume a set of relationships between a particular occupation and notions of public service. The lay person's conception of being professional has its academic counterpart in what is termed the trait theory of professions (Millerson, 1964; Wilensky, 1964). Although the quantity and quality of traits identified can vary, there is a measure of agreement in the literature as to the key traits associated with the idea of a profession (Johnson, 1972). Professions have been identified with ideals of 'public service' (or public interest) and a service ethic. The concept of professionals as 'independent' is closely associated with the public service ideal. It is also commonly assumed that professionals through their studies, training and apprenticeship have developed an understanding of a body of knowledge that most lay people would consider to be abstruse. Finally, a profession is usually assumed to have some state sanctioned control or monopoly over the occupation that is its particular domain.

Although most sociologists of the professions (e.g. Abbott, 1988; Johnson, 1972) would, in our view rightly, consider trait theory an inadequate understanding of the emergence and functioning of professions, including accountancy (cf. Robson and Cooper, 1990), trait theory expresses many aspects of a prevailing discourse concerning professions. For example, the key traits that we identify are clearly evidenced in the writing of histories of the accountancy bodies and the accounting profession in both the UK (Carr-Saunders and Wilson, 1934; Stacey, 1954) and the US (Carey, 1969; 1970; Littleton and Zimmerman, 1962). In such works the roles of accountancy in providing a public service, facilitating the stewardship of assets and mediating the efficient allocation of resources in society have been constant themes (Robson and Cooper, 1990). By extension, the ideals expressed by trait theory contain the self-image that professional institutions wish to project:

trait theory is part of a discourse about professions that is *performative* in that it structures how professions are viewed and how professional bodies and their members project themselves as professional. For example, Cooper *et al* (1996) show how the representatives of the government and the ICAEW deployed such concepts of professionalism as a strategic resource in managing negotiations with the European Commission and its member states on the content and implementation of the Eighth Directive on the regulation of auditors.

Whilst this judgement as to the role of trait theory stresses its positive role in the maintenance of professional autonomy the concept of an ideal profession that it expresses can also mediate criticism of accounting and accountants. Critics of the lack of independence of auditors and accountants (Scott, 1931; Briloff, 1972; Sikka and Willmott, 1995) have targeted the concept of the public service ideal of a profession above that of commercial gain and used this as a basis for questioning the mercantile orientation of the large auditing firms. Other commentators have questioned the nature, quality and depth of the knowledge base of accountancy in ways that suggest a lack of professionalism (Stamp and Marley, 1970). Such judgements have contributed to the call for a Conceptual Framework to protect accountancy's professional integrity (Solomons, 1978; 1986).

In short, the concepts that make up the 'ideal' profession are central to the status and reputation of accountancy in the UK. An important component of the professionalization project - the process of maintaining and furthering the professional identity for the occupation - is achieved by articulating the ideals expressed through the professional discourse which helps the accounting firms maintain certain occupational privileges and is a strategic resource in furthering their activities. Yet the claim to professional status can also serve to structure criticisms of accounting practices and firms in circumstances where certain activities are viewed as moving away from accepted notions of the profession and professional modes of conduct.

For these reasons accounting institutions and member firms have been careful to preserve the notion of themselves as professionals. It is this process that, in part, motivated our study of socialization in auditing firms and the practices through which trainees presumably come to understand the meaning of 'profession' and 'professional'. In the succeeding sections we examine the dimensions of the institutional configuration of accountancy in the UK that mediate in both positive and negative ways the capacity of accountancy's members to maintain an identity with being professionals. We identify three important aspects of this configuration: institutional fragmentation, occupational diversity, and the existence and influence of the large multi-national auditing firms.

1.1 Institutional Fragmentation

The existence of six professional bodies within the UK, each offering training and examination procedures leading to the qualification 'accountant', is revealing of several tensions in the professional identity of accounting. Although several attempts at merger between subsets of the six professional institutes have been attempted in the post-war era, many of them supported by agencies of the British government, only one, between the Institute of Chartered Accountants in England and Wales (ICAEW) and the Society of Incorporated Accountants (SIA), has thus far been successful. This fragmentation at the level of 'professional' association has reflected the variety of organizational sites in which accountants operate: central and local government, corporations, multi-national audit firms, small partnerships, etc. Moreover, it has been a source of irritation to the department of the UK government responsible for regulating accountancy (Willmott *et al*, 1993) that the professional bodies have failed to amalgamate. The resistance to mergers between accountancy bodies has not, however, been solely a function of their differing occupational functions; significant overlaps in the activities of members exist between several accountancy bodies, especially the four bodies (ACCA, ICAEW, ICAI, ICAS) with the authority to undertake statutory audits.

The differing organizational sites and activities (the professional audit partner, the company accountant) partly accounts for the ways in which the professional bodies have accrued different levels of status. For example, the formation of the Institute of Cost and Works Accountants (ICWA, now Chartered Institute of Management Accountants, CIMA) demonstrated how the views of 'gentlemen accountants' of the ICAEW towards employment in industrial organizations provided the social space for low status 'cost clerks' to form their own professional association of cost accountants (Loft, 1986; Jones, 1981). The rejection of the scheme for integration by members of the ICAEW in July 1970 seemingly reflected a view of their relative standing. The four accountancy bodies authorised to perform the 'reserved function', i.e. statutory audit, claimed this monopoly control as a source of superior status.

The ICAEW has by far the strongest historical relationship with the influential agencies of central government, even though the Chartered Institute of Public Finance and Accountancy (CIPFA) has the largest membership in local government and public sector organizations. Partly due to its location in the City of London, its claims to status and its size, the ICAEW has interacted closely, through its Parliamentary and Law Committee, with government on economic issues since the early 1960s.

Holders of the post of Head of the Government Accountancy Service (HOTGAS) have all come from the ICAEW. Other claims to higher status have been founded upon the apparent superiority of accountancy training in (accounting and audit) practice rather than industry, although recent moves to allow qualification 'outside of public practice' have eroded these sources of difference.

1.2 Occupational Diversity

If the existence of six institutes each claiming professional accountancy status has possibly compromised the professional unity of accountancy, it is equally important to recognise that the diversity of 'services' now performed by accountants extends far beyond the activities for which they are formally qualified. Tax advice, insolvency and receiverships, special investigations, management consulting, IT consulting, public sector and privatisation work, legal and financial services are routinely offered by auditing firms in addition to the usual accounting and auditing functions. Moreover, the spread of markets for accounting labour has been reinforced by the acceptance in UK business of an accountancy qualification as, seemingly, a general qualification in management. As well as having one of the highest densities of accountants per capita of any nation in the world, the UK has also a much higher proportion of accountants occupying senior management positions (Horowitz, 1978).

　　If the success of accountancy in colonising markets in which its members have no necessary competencies or professional training demonstrates successful market action on the part of accounting firms, it is also a significant source of tension in the accounting coalition. In the past decade signs have emerged of increasing tensions in the capacity of accountancy bodies to speak for their members (Cooper *et al*, 1996). Often such tensions have emerged out of the very entrepreneurial success of accountants in colonising new markets not obviously connected to perceptions of accounting expertise. For example, the growth of accounting and auditing practices offering a range of financial services brought many within the regulatory net of the 1986 Financial Services Act. This in turn led to the creation of the Joint Monitoring Unit by the professional bodies and the advent of pro-active monitoring and inspection of accounting firms providing financial services. This and other extensions of the regulatory field of the accountancy bodies have not been popular among their members. The disparate activities of the group collectively labelled accountants provided the basis for the setting up of the Tricker (1983) and Worsley (1985) Reports into the organization and structure of the ICAEW (Sikka and Willmott, 1995). Problems in securing the consent of members in agreeing to accounting regulations (such as the inflation accounting standards) and fee increases have been recurrent (Davison, 1987).

Other sources of stress have emerged between the Big Six audit firms and the small practitioners, and the relationship of both constituents to their accountancy institutes. The Tricker Report (1983) presented an image of senior partners of Big Six firms who were no longer so concerned to become involved in the work of the ICAEW. Accountants in small firms, by contrast, were believed to see the ICAEW as dominated by the national and global interests of the Big Six. The particular situation of the Big Six embodies many of these and other tensions in accountancy's professional claim.

1.3 The Multi-National Auditing 'Industry'

The position of the large multi-national auditing firms, providing the full range of accounting, auditing and non-accounting services, illustrates many of the tensions that now operate upon accountancy as a result of occupational diversity. Although audit continues to be an important part of the portfolio of work undertaken by the Big Six it is a declining proportion of their activities. Although there was significant growth in demand for audit services in the post-war era, this growth has been curtailed in recent years and the prospect for future expansion of this area of work in this area is not good. The rise in the number of claims against the large auditing firms for negligent audit work has led to some questioning by the large audit firms of the structure of their organization. As Hopwood *et al* (1990) have noted, this is likely to lead to further divisionalization within Big Six firms as they seek to limit their professional liability and seek further specialization in services to clients.

The level of professional indemnity premiums is already a major concern to audit firms. Moreover, the increase in litigation against large audit firms suggests that the obligations of auditing firms towards third parties may be increasing, which would make audit, a core service of the profession, less economically attractive.

Changes in the political environment continue to have an effect upon the professional standing of accountancy. For example, the idea that the profession should owe a duty of care to detect fraud is not yet accepted by the accountancy bodies themselves but is suggestive of a wider lack of faith in the perceived independence of auditors. Although the UK has yet to have the type of inquiry into auditor independence and the large audit firms undertaken in the US, such as those of Metcalfe and Dingell, some British Members of Parliament and academics have begun to question the role of the accountancy bodies in terms suggesting that professional status is not taken for granted (Cousins and Sikka, 1993; Cousins *et al*, 1993). The involvement of large audit firms in public sector issues such as National Health Service management and Local Management of Schools (LMS) has brought accounting and auditing practices into areas of organizational and social life previously governed by forms of consensus politics and the professional norms of other occupations. Although the large accounting firms are keen to stress the technical nature of their interventions into public sector management, it is possible to view such work as leading to a perception of the politicisation of accounting practices incommensurable with the independence of professionals (Hopwood *et al*, 1990, pp.46-47). Academic studies of monopolistic concentration in the market for auditors (Simunic, 1980) reflect concerns about the economic strength of the Big Six. Other debates have focused upon the level of influence exerted by the large firms on the processes of accounting standard setting and on whose behalf that influence has been exercised (Hussein and Ketz, 1980; Haring, 1979).

Viewed as 'industries', the economic scale and scope of Big Six auditing firms are now considerable. For example, in the present study Firm B currently employs around 80,000 staff and administrators world-wide of whom 35,000 are located in Europe. The annual global turnover of Firm B was almost $6 billion in 1995. The commercial significance of the multi-national auditing bodies has not been lost on the government agencies responsible for sponsoring the accounting profession. The potential to extend the earnings potential of the large auditing firms has structured the negotiating stances of the British government during the development of EU Directives on Company Law (Cooper *et al*, 1996). Indeed concerns about the independence of auditors led the European Commission to suggest restrictions on the activities of audit firms in its Eighth Directive on Company Law. As an official of the Department of Trade and Industry explained to one of the present authors in the context of a discussion on the shape of the Eighth EC Directive:

"There are more accountants than steelworkers in the UK" (Robson *et al*, 1994, p.512).

Such a large scale corporate environment may suggest an erosion of the linkages between the qualified accountant and the ideals of a profession with which he or she is purported to identify. Although the Senior Partners of the multi-national auditing firms would be cautious in endorsing such a view, the sociologist of professions Andrew Abbott has commented that the allegiance of the Big Six qualified accountants is to the firm first and the profession second (Abbott, 1988, p.154). Given that the partnership structure of accounting and audit firms has often been defended as the appropriate model for professional practices, recent moves by certain Big Six firms towards incorporation of some of their core business could be interpreted as a further loosening of the ties of professionalism even if the motivation for such moves has more to do with the costs of professional indemnity insurance and the rise in negligence suits against auditors. The 1989 Companies Act permitted incorporated firms to act as auditors, subject to certain requirements. As incorporation of audit firms would imply some form of public scrutiny in terms of accounting regulations, this may explain why there was no immediate take up of this option. However, with fears about audit liability, the large audit firms may set up an incorporated entity for their audit services.

In summary, the socialization of accounting professionals occurs in an extremely complex social context in which the ideal of an allegiance to the 'profession' is highly problematic. Accountants are, in some senses differentiated by:

- the institutes to which they belong;
- their organizational environments;
- the nature of their work practices;
- the size and scope of their firm; and
- the status they and other accountants attach to their work.

In this context it could be argued that the question of an identification with the ideals of a profession, the accountancy profession, is crucial; where there are so many potential lines of division the professional identity might or should assume more importance. On the other hand, the context we have outlined could be suggestive of a gradual process of de-professionalization: the notion of a unitary profession, and its associated ideals, may have little practical or symbolic meaning to the accountant or auditor. In this scenario there may be emerging either a gradual disregard for any residual notions of professional traits and norms or the term profession assumes simply an instrumental value for accountants in increasing the prices they can charge for their services to clients.

In the next section we develop the theoretical context to this by examining the conceptual studies of professionalization that have been developed with particular emphasis upon the issue of professional socialization and the case of accountancy. In the first section, however, we outline the main theoretical approaches to the study of professions.

2. The Study of Professions

The role of the professions in Anglo-American society has been explored by writers since the turn of the century (e.g. Spencer, 1914). Systematic theoretical investigation of what the professions are, how they come to be and how they successfully maintain their professional status is generally acknowledged, however, as beginning after World War II. Although by the early 1980s it was claimed that the professions were no longer of interest to sociologists (Hall 1983), changes in the world of work and the activities of the professions over the last decade or so have led to the acknowledgement of the need to focus on the professions once again (cf. Freidson, 1994).

Although many theoretical and empirical strands to research on professions exist, including Marxist, Weberian, trait and functionalist approaches (Johnson, 1972; Larson, 1977), within the sociology of the professions there is a body of research that concentrates on the role of the education, training, and induction experiences of professionals. These works acknowledge the importance of the formal learning process that facilitates the acquisition and application of certain technical or esoteric knowledge. This knowledge is, *inter alia*, essential for professional success at both the individual and institutional levels. Such studies also highlight the importance of learning more broadly how to be a member of a certain profession. The process of adopting the values, norms and behaviours of the profession is vital for professional success. Demonstration of these characteristics permits group membership for the individual professional and acts as a sign of that group membership to those outside the profession. Consequently, an individual's incorporation of the values and norms of a profession into their identity and repertoire of behaviours is just as vital to successfully becoming a professional as the formal education process and achievement of the professional qualification.

This process which involves individuals learning to conform to prevalent norms is termed *socialization*. Socialization takes place from an early stage in life and, at a general level, is envisaged as having three stages. The first stage occurs as the child learns how to fit into its family, the second stage refers to when the child enters school and is faced with a new wider environment and the third stage is adult socialization whereby individuals learn first-hand what it is to be an employee, a spouse, a parent, etc. Professional socialization is one aspect of adult socialization which is required of those people wishing to become formally recognised as a member of a profession including professionals working within organizations. The latter are therefore subject to a dual process of professional and organizational socialization.

It is within the study of professionalization, that is of how occupational groups come to be professions and how they maintain their status as professional groups, that the importance of socialization becomes clear. In the next section of this chapter we aim to provide an introduction and overview to the sociology of the professions, and professional and organizational socialization, thus 'locating' the research reported in this book.

3. The Sociology of the Professions

The concept of profession was not systematically explored until the expansion of academic sociology after Word War II (Freidson, 1994). The first attempts at theorising the professions in the English-speaking world emanated from America (for example, Talcott Parsons, 1951; 1964; 1968 and Everett Hughes, 1958). Parsons explored the contradictions existing between the notions of altruism claimed by the professions and the model of self-interest that is central to economic theory and utilitarianism; in so doing Parsons endeavoured to link the 'functions' of the professions to the maintenance of social and economic order. Functionalist theories, influenced by the works of Durkheim, aimed to determine how particular groups/structures/institutions serve the needs of society and sustain harmonious integration. The functionalist approach held that the professions are distinctive from other occupational groups and that a profession is a group that has a high degree of homogeneity and consensus. Durkheim claimed:

> "that the professions were a precondition of consensus in industrial societies, and that the break-up of the traditional moral order initiated by the fragmenting division of labour would be rectified only by the formation of moral communities based upon occupational membership" (Johnson, 1972, p.12).

Consequently the trait approach, which focuses on determining the ideal-typical profession so that occupational groups can be assessed against these criteria, is strongly associated with the functionalist approach. Indeed the traits of altruism and collectivity orientation (Parsons, 1954), which may still influence many people's expectations of professionals, were central to many trait-approach studies. Hughes (1958) analyzed the features of professions in order to highlight what the professions had in common with other occupations with a view to breaking down some of the mystique that surrounded the professions. Linked to these models of individual self-interest and social goals, the work of Wilensky (1964), Goode (1969) and Moore (1970) aimed to document regularities in the historical achievement of professional status, in order to ascertain the unique characteristics of those occupations that are or become professions. Such theories of professions came to be characterized as trait theories in that they sought to identify and enumerate the key or 'essential' characteristics that all professions share, albeit professions that seemed to be confined to the Anglo-American context. As Johnson (1972) and many others writers on the theory of professions have noted (Abbott, 1988; Freidson, 1972; Larson, 1977) such work singularly failed to consider the dynamic character of the process of becoming a profession (professionalization) and how such occupations maintain their professional status in changing social contexts.

The 1960s saw a change in the character of writings on the professions and professionalization. Whilst the predominant explanations of the existence of professionals were functionalist in that they held that the professions existed because they were serving the needs of society, the 'revisionist' histories of the professions that were produced in this period introduced the era of critical studies of the professions (e.g. Platt, 1969; Rothman, 1971; Auerbach, 1976). These studies reported that the policies of the professions were indicative of the professions' economic self-interest and status concerns, and described how the activities of the professions 'facilitated control of the poor, the working class, and the deviant' (Freidson, 1994, p.3). That is, rather than serving some pre-existing needs of society the professions actively define the needs of society and determine what sort of service consumers/clients receive. Indeed by the 1970s this focus on power and conflict had become the dominant perspective. For example, Freidson (1970, 1970b):

"emphasized the ideological character of professional claims, unjustified aspects of monopolistic privilege, and the way organized professional institutions create and sustain authority over clients, associated occupations, and the very way we think about deviant or undesirable behaviour" (Freidson, 1994).

A similarly critical vein in sociological studies of professions was introduced by the Marxist analysis of Terry Johnson (1972) who defined professionalism as a method of occupational control in which the consumer is subordinated to the producer. In 1977 Larson, utilising Marxist and Weberian theory, defined professionalization, that is the process of becoming a profession, as a 'collective mobility project' and the professions as interest groups linked to the class system.

Freidson (1970) and Johnson (1972) highlighted the role of knowledge within the professions, by analysing how the production and reproduction of knowledge, or expertise, is essential for the power of a profession. Freidson held that professionalism is located both in the ideology and everyday conduct of occupational groups and structurally in terms of the functional autonomy allowed the profession by the state, i.e. the profession has exclusive right to control access to, and organize, the tasks which it performs. Although Dingwall (1976) criticised Freidson's claim that all professions have functional autonomy in common, a focus on the combination of espoused ideology, everyday conduct of professionals, and legal frameworks has remained a common component of studies of professionalization.

Until the 1970s medicine had been the prime focus of attention for researchers interested in the professions and consequently served as the primary model for conceptualising professionalism (Freidson, 1994). Studies since then, however, have looked to other professions (e.g. law and engineering) and to non English-speaking countries to widen the understanding of the professions and professionalization. These comparative studies have, amongst other things, in turn increasingly highlighted the role of the State in successful professionalization (e.g. Halliday, 1989).

Marxist theory of professions has been concerned with the degree to which the professions are a product of the division of labour and aimed to demonstrate the secondary and derivative character of the professions, particularly with regard to their negative contribution to surplus value (Johnson, 1972, p.10). More recent Marxist sociology of the professions is essentially concerned with the professions in relation to the state (e.g. Johnson 1980) and the proletarianization of professional occupations (e.g. Derber, 1982; Haug, 1988).

Weber's concepts of social stratification and social closure have been of importance to authors such as Larkin (1983), Waddington (1984) and Macdonald (1984; 1985; 1989). Moreover, the definition of society as individuals pursuing individual interests is central to Larson's (1977) influential concept of the 'professional project', itself developed from the work of Freidson. Macdonald (1995) claims this concept to be the most useful means of understanding the professions:

"Professionalization is thus an attempt to translate one order of scarce resources - special knowledge and skills - into another - social and economic rewards. To maintain scarcity implies a tendency to monopoly: monopoly of expertise in the market, monopoly of status in a system of stratification. The focus on the constitution of professional markets leads to comparing different professions in terms of the 'marketability' of their specific cognitive resources" (Larson quoted in Macdonald, 1995, p.9).

Professions are groups of individuals who come together to further their own interests and in the course of this quest for collective social mobility they aim to exclude others from their group and take the privileges of other groups. This restriction of access to rewards which yields maximization of a particular group's advantage via exclusion and/or usurpation is described by Weber's term *social closure*. Consequently Macdonald states that the "overall strategy of a professional group is best understood in terms of social closure" (Macdonald, 1995, p.35). Macdonald then goes on to state that:

"Sociologists who are closer to Weber than to Marx would argue that the realities of social stratification require the analysis of 'social closure' based not only on property in the means of production but on other criteria as well (Collins, 1975; 1979; 1981; Murphy, 1988; Parkin, 1979)" (Macdonald, 1995, p.50).

The most important of these criteria is '*credentialism*' (the allocation of occupational positions on the basis of educational qualifications) which has become central to the collective social mobility of the professions (Hughes, 1971; Macdonald, 1995).

Whilst much of the sociology of the professions, and research on professional education and socialization, had been dominated by the trait approach and the Functionalist paradigm, the emergence of Marxist, Weberian and Symbolic Interactionist approaches reflected a new diversity in theories of professions (Coffey, 1993, p.41). Although both Marxist and Weberian theories denied the role of professions as being to fulfil pre-given social or economic needs in society, the Symbolic Interactionist approach went further in disputing the claim of Marxist and Weberian theories that there were *necessarily* relationships of occupational power, state sanction or economic domination that characterise all professions. Atkinson (1981, p.8) summarised the opposing viewpoints between Symbolic Interactionist and other theories thus:

"In simple terms one can identify two competing approaches: one which seeks to identify 'professions' as distinctive, special sorts of occupations, and one which denies any inherent qualities which might set them apart [Symbolic Interactionism]".

Symbolic Interactionism, inspired by the Chicago school of sociology, focuses on the everyday, small-scale interactions that reveal how people negotiate situations and roles and gain a social identity. Symbolic Interactionism does not view the professions as necessarily different from other occupations. The focus of studies in this tradition is not the "abstract standard which characterises a formal collectivity" (Macdonald, 1995, p.4) but the day-to-day aspects of life and work. In this way Symbolic Interactionist theory underlines the recognition that it is not only the technical knowledge base of professional expertise that is used, via credentialism, within the profession's tactic of social closure, an insight that is at the basis of our first thesis in this study. In the work of Dingwall (1979) learning the 'correct' behaviours and norms is seen to be crucial in presenting the correct image to clients and other professionals - a professional has to know how to convey the impression that their service and its practitioners are 'special', thus allowing people outside the profession to place the practitioner within that special group and themselves outside of the group. Dingwall identified this 'accomplishing profession' when investigating the training and education of health visitors in the UK:

> "The accomplishment of health visiting as a 'profession' involves its members in being certain kinds of people who carry out tasks in particular ways within a particular work setting" (Dingwall, 1979, p.340).

Indeed in this study Dingwall notes that:

> "Academic ability is not enough. Student assessment is an evaluation of the total person as revealed in everyday activities" (Dingwall, 1979, p.337).

These qualities required of the health visitor were consequently noted as a fundamental part of health visitor training. Part of being a professional involves a regulation of the self in terms of the articulation of a professional discourse, the following of formal and informal norms of conduct: in short, the expectation of appropriate and social behaviour from oneself and from others. Likewise the clients of a profession and the general public expect certain behaviours too. It is these informal or behavioural aspects to the 'making up' of accounting professionals that we explore in this book.

Abbott (1988) extended the Interactionists concern with demonstrating how professionalism is negotiated on a day-to-day basis by showing how the professions collectively determine their existence through negotiation with society at various levels. Abbott holds that it is the work that professions do that separates them as an occupational group, not their organizational structure and its historical development. Professions are those occupational groups that perform work that has as its base abstract knowledge that is perceived to be of use by members of the society the profession belongs to. Yet rather than moving into vacant slots in society these occupational groups are actively involved in the construction and definition of the knowledge and 'problems' that accompany it. Having established social/cultural legitimacy for their expertise the occupational group then claims jurisdiction:

> "In claiming jurisdiction, a profession asks society to recognize its cognitive structure through exclusive rights; jurisdiction has not only a culture, but also a social structure. These claimed rights may include absolute monopoly of practice and of public payments, rights of self-discipline and of unconstrained employment, control of professional training, of recruitment and of licensing, to mention only a few" (Abbott, 1988, p.59).

Abbott frames this claim of jurisdiction within a competitive system, whereby all jurisdictions, and the demise and creation of jurisdictions, impact on other jurisdictions (i.e. professions). Survival is by no means assured once a jurisdiction is successfully claimed. The claims must be maintained and developed formally within the legal and public arenas and informally at the workplace.

Consequently recent research into professions suggests that learning the values, behaviour, and knowledge required to become a member of a chosen profession are vital at the individual level for those wishing to become a qualified professional person. If a person fails to do so it is unlikely that they will be successful in their career as both clients and colleagues will be dissatisfied with individual performance. In addition, as the professions have to maintain their status and jurisdictions in order to continue to exist as professions the behavioural/value requirements imposed on a profession's members by the profession and by its clients and culture are paramount. Their reproduction in or negotiation by, each new member, and their collective development in light of the changing demands of society and the profession, are essential for the continued success of the profession. So whilst the market project involving exclusion and/or usurpation is essential so too is what Freidson refers to as the 'maintenance project' which involves:

> "maintaining sufficient cohesion of the profession as a whole to be able to undertake common action both to sustain its status and privilege and to advance its own 'cultural' projects" (Freidson, 1994, p.202).

Freidson states that several things contribute to the maintenance of cohesion/common identities:

- relative to other occupations, professionals have a distinct public identity;
- common socialization as a result of college education and training experiences; and

- as a result of the 'sunk cost' of lengthy training procedures most professionals commit themselves to a life-long career in the profession.

In addition:

> "A critical but often ignored method of sustaining the solidarity of the profession lies in the norms governing relations among its members and lay people. They may be written as rules or practised as unwritten custom" (Freidson, 1994, p.203).

These norms, amongst other things, affect competitive behaviour and relations between professionals and clients. This aspect of becoming, and being, a professional is crucial to some sense of professional cohesion and it is upon these processes that socialization studies focus.

4. Professional and Organizational Socialization

As noted earlier, socialization, a term employed in sociology and psychology, is the process of learning the appropriate way of doing things, of learning how to be in a certain environment, of internalising the norms, values and beliefs of a culture. The term is synonymous with 'enculturation' (Olesen and Whittaker, 1970). All cultures encourage some behaviour whilst discouraging other behaviour. Studies of professional and organizational socialization consequently aim to explore the formal training programmes undertaken by new members and their day-to-day experience in order to profile what values, knowledge and behaviour are encouraged and how this is achieved.

Whilst anyone starting a new job in a new organization must learn how to do their task and how to fit into the new organization, the degree to which this knowledge will remain crucial to their career success is variable. The training of people wanting to achieve professional status and achieve career success by using their professional status must, however, serve them well for their future posts. New members of a profession have to learn the academic and technical aspects of the expertise that is central to their profession. They also have to learn the 'correct' way to act and think, and the values that should be espoused, within the wider environment of their chosen profession. The values and behaviours learnt in this formative period are likely to remain with the individual in years to come. This is achieved, however, within a certain training environment and so their learning process will be intermingled with learning how to survive in that particular training environment. That professional socialization will also involve organizational socialization is most obvious in cases where training is undertaken on-the-job, as is the case with training contracts within accountancy. The degree to which organizational and professional socialization are separable will be explored in Chapter 5. The next section aims to summarise the main historical developments in the study of professional socialization, with a view to illustrating the different perspectives on what is central to this process.

4.1 Professional Socialization

Functionalist and Symbolic Interactionist approaches differ not only in how they define the professions, but also in how they see the learning processes undertaken by professionals. The Functionalist perspective tends to focus on the characteristics of the occupation that new members must learn:

> "The success or failure of 'becoming' is coached in terms of trainees learning and internalizing easily discernible values and traits. Hence the process of professional socialization is a fixed and objective one" (Coffey, 1993, p.4).

The institution charged with socializing the new professional (be it medical school, accountancy firm etc.) teaches the trainee how to become a professional and the trainee absorbs the values and traits presented to her/him. Symbolic Interactionism on the other hand:

> "focuses upon how people are moulded and shaped by social institutions, while simultaneously negotiating and creating their own professional identities (Bucher and Stelling 1977)" (Coffey, 1993, pp.44-45).

Two seminal works on professional socialization can be contrasted to illustrate the differences between the two approaches. Merton *et al* (1957) and Becker *et al* (1961) studied the training of medical students. However they had different perspectives. Merton *et al* can be placed within the Functionalist tradition and Becker *et al* adopted a broadly Interactionist approach. The picture painted of medical student life differs considerably, as Atkinson notes:

> "The Columbia [Merton] research describes student culture as comprising a 'little society' in which the professional norms of the faculty are reflected and reinforced. At Kansas [Becker], the student culture appears almost to be an 'underground resistance movement', in which students unite against a hostile and threatening environment" (Atkinson, 1981, p.9).

Becker *et al's* illustration of the distinction between the perspectives of those involved in training the would-be professionals and the trainees themselves could be usefully noted by all involved in the training process. Becker *et al* (1961) describes how the values of 'experience' and 'responsibility' are assimilated by medical students. Experience and responsibility are central values of the medical profession. The hierarchical structures of the hospitals reflect the importance of these values as it is the level of each of these that an individual physician has obtained that matters for recognition and career success. Students are faced with a very significant amount of 'book-learning' when they enter medical school and consequently have to decide how best to direct their energy during training. Consequently they take their cues from their environment and the students aim to maximise their 'experience' of a variety of clinical situations and demonstrate their ability to perform those tasks that require some degree of skill, and therefore trust on the part of the superior (i.e. 'responsibility'). As Becker points out, however, the worlds of the student and the qualified physician are not the same and consequently "the meanings they attach to such key concepts as responsibility and experience also differ" (Becker *et al*, 1961, p.270). For the physician they are qualities s/he has and must exercise; for the student they are scarce commodities. Consequently if faculty are unaware of the importance to students of these scarce commodities, and are therefore unaware that the student will be consequently directing most of their energy at gaining this practical experience, they will not be able to make sense of the reluctance of students to take part in other experiences that faculty may believe to be more important, nor will they grasp the sense of resentment that accompanies occasions that deny students opportunities to gain experience and demonstrate responsibility. Therefore, it is clear that attention to the various perspectives of those involved is essential for anyone wishing to understand how any training process is working.

After the studies of Merton and Becker, others studies of professional socialization continued to be undertaken (e.g. Olesen and Whittaker, 1968; Miller, 1970; Mumford, 1970; Hans and Shaffir, 1977), and although the early work on the professions was American there is now a significant UK literature (e.g. Atkinson, 1981; Bunton, 1985; Melia, 1987; Parry, 1988). As we suggested above, while Freidson and Johnson highlighted the importance of knowledge within the professions, Atkinson (1983, p.234) noted that studies of professional socialization were lacking "an adequate treatment of cultural transmission and knowledge management in the reproduction of the professions". More studies of professions have attempted to address this gap: socialization studies have begun to attend to knowledge and its production and reproduction within the professions. Coffey (1993) states that these studies have combined a Symbolic Interactionist perspective with a consideration of professional knowledge, the sociology of the curriculum and the 'new sociology of education'.

Although, as mentioned earlier, Hall (1983) proclaimed that the professions were no longer meaningful to sociologists, and Atkinson (1981; 1983) argued that the professional socialization as a research area was no longer interesting, this focus on the process of knowledge acquisition within the professions has rekindled interest in the area (Coffey, 1993, p.52). Various studies in the UK have focused on professional socialization in recent years, covering areas as diverse as psychiatric training (Bunton, 1985); nursing (Melia, 1987); army recruits (Hockey, 1986); police training (Fielding, 1988) and trainee journalists (Parry, 1988). Consequently Coffey concludes:

> "It is no longer the case that the field is stale, rather it seems to be alive and expanding, both in the terms of the occupational groups studied, and the attention to questions of knowledge production, interpretation and transmission" (Coffey, 1993, p.52).

The inclusion of gender as a research theme within socialization, and the recognition that there are professions other than the traditional 'liberal' professions to be researched are also notable additions to the research area of recent years.

Bucher and Strauss (1961) point out that assuming homogeneity within the professions, and the training (formal and informal) individuals receive, as in the Functionalist tradition, is misleading. In fact, they suggest that there are often several identities, values and interests within professions and hence they are segmented rather than homogenous. Fragmentation within the professions is indeed the focus of attention of observers of professionals. Freidson notes:

> "...attention has focused on the possible consequences of changes within the professions themselves, such as increasing numbers of practitioners and greater internal stratification and fragmentation into specialities, not to speak also of the influence of consumer movements. All analysts agree that in virtually every industrial nation the professions are going through important changes. Marxist analysts predictably forecast proletarianization; others prophesy considerable reorganization of the professions, if not actual loss of their status" (Freidson, 1994, p.4).

Consequently, an analysis of professional socialization and the concepts of professional identity that are constructed during the socialization process is not only of academic interest.

4.2 Organizational Socialization

Studies of professional socialization investigate the nature of professions and highlight how individuals are 'shaped' into members of those particular professions, via experience of training, education and induction. Contained within professional socialization is the experience of organizational socialization. That is, individuals experience their chosen profession within an organizational environment.

As organizational socialization and professional socialization are interrelated to various degrees, rather than attempt to summarise the developments in this wider field of study it is more useful to look at some of the general findings of the organizational studies with a view to exploring how they may affect the professional socialization experience.

Socialization occurs in a variety of ways. Formal procedures such as recruitment, appraisal and training, and informal advice and observation of others, provide the newcomer with information on how to behave and give rise to situations in which existing members of the organization may attempt to shape the behaviour and values of the newcomer. Feldman (1981) conceptualized the socialization of organization members as consisting of three areas of change:

"1. socialization as the acquisition of a set of appropriate role behaviours;
2. socialization as the development of work skills and abilities;
3. socialization as adjustment to the work group's norms and values"
(Feldman, 1981, p.309).

He located these aspects of socialization in three temporal phases: 'anticipatory socialization', which refers to experience gained and values held prior to joining the organization; 'encounter' when the new member of the organization starts to get a 'true' picture of the organization; and 'change and acquisition' where the socialization process can be seen to have led to long-lasting and 'satisfactory' changes. Feldman proposed process variables for each socialization phase which he suggests the new member must be achieving successfully:

- At Anticipatory Socialization: Realism about the organization; Realism about the job; Congruence of skills and abilities; Congruence of needs and values.
- At Encounter: Management of outside-life conflicts; Management of inter-group role conflicts; Role definition; Initiation to the task; Initiation to the group.
- At Change and Acquisition: Resolution of role demands; Task mastery; Adjustment to group norms and values.

Feldman's model, whether one agrees with the classifications and stages or not, provides a powerful illustration of just how much is involved in learning a new job in a new organization. He also provides a useful warning that:

> "recruits will resist attempts to change their values and attitudes when their sense of self-control and self-determination is threatened" (Feldman, 1981, p.314).

If it is assumed that the organization wants its members to be committed to their job, and the organization, and to perform their job/role as well as they can, whilst adhering to values such as efficiency, client service, and flexibility then the processes by which commitment is generated needs careful attention. The use of symbolism and the value of corporate culture have been well documented over the past decade or so (e.g. Peters and Waterman, 1982). Those organizations which use these non-physical means to construct boundaries between members of the organization and non-members can be thought of as 'greedy institutions' (Coser, 1974) as they aim to work on, and possess, the whole person. Each organization varies, to some degree, in respect of its values and operating procedures. In this way the new professional will be shaped, to some degree, according to the character of the organization. Consequently if a profession has members socialized in a diverse number of environments it may be the case that the professional emerging from one environment is quite different to the professional emerging from another training environment.

If one takes the perspective of the newcomer it is easy to see that attempts to change one's values, one's appearance, and how one spends one's time (e.g. at work vs. non-work activities) may be quite to difficult to accept. Recruitment processes aim to reduce the friction that may be felt at this stage by selecting people who, *inter alia*, seem to be the 'right' sort of person already, who are for example, committed to working hard, and who have a positive view of the company already.

Regardless of careful selection procedures the phenomenon of 'reality shock' is well documented. Reality shock has often been used to refer to the experience of making the transition from school to work (Wagneschein, 1950; Becker, 1952). In general terms, however, it refers to any discrepancy between the expectations that an individual had prior to joining an organization and their perceptions on becoming a member of that organization, and as a social-psychological concept it posits that this discrepancy leads to an experience of 'stress'. Dean (1983) states that reality shock comes about as a result of the socialization process and Dean *et al* (1988) suggest that reality shock actually affects the organizational commitment of members: the greater the reality shock, the less commitment.

As a new member of an organization, an individual will have expectations about what the organization will do for them and what they will do for the organization. Eisenberger *et al* (1986) suggest that organizational commitment is based on beliefs that the organization will meet an individual's emotional and economic needs. Zaccaro and Dobbins (1989) report that organizational commitment has a different psychological basis to group commitment within the organization and that it is indeed the likes of met expectations and satisfaction with promotion chances (i.e. those aspects of organizational experience that relate to positive social exchange) that characterise the basis of organizational commitment rather than liking one's group members and perceptions of group cohesiveness and so on. Consequently the early experiences of members of organizations are crucial in terms of future behaviour and satisfaction, and it may be inferred from these findings that the early experiences of a profession must likewise aim to minimise the 'painful' aspects of reality shock. One aspect of reality shock that may or may not affect willingness to stay in the profession is the shift from idealism to cynicism that is documented by writers on the professions. Becker and Geer (1960) and Becker *et al* (1961) describe how medical students soon forget their idealistic views about medicine and adopt an approach that focuses on doing whatever it takes to get through medical school. Similar points have been made about other groups of professional trainees, including accountants (Harper, 1988).

Studies of organizational socialization have also examined the two aspects of socialization that are regarded as central to success in the organization: the management of self-presentation, and the (ritual aspects of) time-management.

4.2.1 Self-Presentation Having the 'correct' image can be seen as essential to fitting-in and demonstrating commitment to the organization or profession.

Some organizations such as the military or religious orders actually issue a standard uniform and strip away, as it were, the previous identity of the new member (e.g. Hockey 1986, Campbell-Jones 1979). As noted earlier, the presentation of the self to clients and other professionals is a central element of professionalism (Dingwall, 1976). Consequently organizations not only demand a certain image as indication of commitment to the organization but certain organizations demand that an image is maintained for the sake of professionalism. Indeed as Coffey notes in her study of an accounting firm:

> "The organization relays to the students 'appropriate' self presentation skills, both formally and informally through role modelling, ridicule and expectation. The occupational group may also operate with a particular notion of self presentation forming part of a salient characteristic or trait of what it is to be a 'professional' doctor, lawyer, accountant and so on" (Coffey, 1993, p.68).

In this way the organization's practices influence the self-presentation, or image, of its professionals.

4.2.2 Time-Management   Dandridge (1986) has suggested that the management of time has symbolic and real value for organizations. Procedures for time-management could indeed be seen to reflect various values such as punctuality, trust, commitment, flexibility. Of course, commitment to an organization is also often measured (informally if not formally) in terms of time given to the organization. Learning when it is acceptable to leave work, if it is acceptable to take a long lunch-break, if it is possible to have a personal life etc. are some of the fundamental lessons in the socialization process.

The training and early experience in general of an organization and profession are central to the development of professional knowledge and identity. This chapter has elucidated the complex nature of the process such that the value of an analysis of what is taught and what is learned is clear. The following, and final, section of this chapter illustrates the concepts and processes described above by detailing the findings of the limited number of previous studies of socialization within the accountancy profession.

5. The Socialization of Accountants

There has been remarkably little study of the recruitment, training and socialization of accountants. Harper (1988), Power (1991), Dirsmith *et al*

(1997), Grey (1994; 1998) and Hanlon (1994) are partial exceptions, but Coffey's PhD thesis, *Double Entry: The Professional and Organizational Socialization of Graduate Accountants* (1993) is the most detailed existing study. Indeed as Hanlon (1994, p.82) points out "sociology has never been enthusiastic in its examination of the work of accountants".

However, Macdonald (1995) concluded his book *The Sociology of the Professions* with a case study of accountancy in order to illustrate the concept of 'professional project' which is the central concept within his writing. In particular, he concludes the chapter with a reference to the importance of those qualities associated with socialization:

> "The minutiae of personal conduct and appearance might seem unimportant but in fact they are as crucial as the firm's procedures and proformas that guide an auditor through the daily work, or the process for the selection and training of staff. Great care is taken to get the right work performed, in the right way, by the right people, wearing the right clothes. Of such stuff is the garment of professionalism made: and such is the display of knowledge and trustworthiness that justifies monopoly" (Macdonald, 1995, p.207).

Hanlon (1994) stated that the accountant's training is centred on developing 'business virtue' as commercialism demands that the 'professional' qualities of the accountant are exercised for the benefit of the client (and not the public). He asserted that as clients demand the best advice achieving technical expertise is obviously a factor in training but other matters such as presentation, the ability not to antagonise clients, capability to reach the right conclusions (as set down by management), ability to uphold the practice's 'good name' are qualities that trainee accountants have to learn to acquire. Hanlon also argued that as the work of trainees is routine there is a 'relative lack of importance attached to the work carried out by trainees' other than speed and efficiency. Indeed, Hanlon claimed that one of the main ways of 'distinguishing' trainees is their personality - their 'general friendliness'.

The formal assessment systems in place in firms and the emphasis on promotion are cited by Hanlon as constitutive of 'an atmosphere of competitive individualism', which guides trainees towards exhibiting the required behaviours (Hanlon, 1994, p.113): the focus on the individual rather than the collectivity is seen as illustrative of a fundamental value of accountancy. Similarly, in his study of the ICAEW professional examinations Power concluded that the continual assessment and mock examinations with the scores posted at the back of the classroom for all to see:

"creates a very literal form of (glowing) visibility in relation to one's contemporaries and thereby an understated but nevertheless real atmosphere of competition" (Power, 1991, p.341).

Power also suggests that the style of teaching and examination encourages trainees to value: speed, relevance, neatness of presentation and systematicity, but not understanding (1991, p.340).

In her research into the socialization of accountants Coffey (1993) followed the progress of ten graduates in the first-year of their three-year training contracts with an international accountancy firm ('Western Ridge'). She also noted the role of competition in the socialization of the trainees. For example, she argued that as their training progressed the trainees are seen to become more competitive, and, indeed, recognise this characteristic themselves. This competitive spirit is facilitated by the significance placed upon the idea of 'the group' by the firm and the tutors. In this way the individual members experienced a sense of pressure not to let the other group members down by doing badly in examinations, but at the same time as wanting the group to succeed individuals (some more than others) want to be the best, that is they sought to be perceived as 'group leader'. This focus on collective identity was also facilitated by "the hard sell techniques of the firm - which emphasised specific organizational identity". That is the trainees were made very aware that they were being trained to be 'Western Ridge' accountants, not just accountants.

Zaccaro and Dobbins (1989) argued that group commitment and organizational commitment are different things, with organizational commitment based upon perceptions of the organization meeting expectations. This is illustrated well by the fate of the trainees, as described by Coffey. By the end of their first-year most of the trainees were classed as a "bad year" by the personnel and managers in the firm with several of them having received poor appraisals of their training and work performance. Accordingly four trainees were not promoted, which was apparently unusual in the firm. One trainee resigned early and another did so at the end of the first year. The trainees had had what was regarded as less audit experience than previous years. This caused resentment, partly in view of the trainees' own consensus that they had not received relevant audit experiences but had been required to undertake many menial tasks such as photo-copying. The issue was not merely boredom, but self-image and progression to professional identity, as one trainee commented:

"Some of us are still students, others can now really call themselves accountants. I'm still a student" (Coffey, 1993, p.461).

Although trainees felt unhappy at the way the non-promotions were handled, Coffey noted that this, combined with the lack of 'good' work, had the effect of strengthening the group and their widespread disillusionment with the firm:

> "The overriding emotions were feelings of being let down by Western Ridge, the dilution or disappearance of respect the trainees had for the firm and the absence of loyalty to the firm" (Coffey, 1993, p.494).

Despite this lack of work and general resentment amongst trainees Coffey points out the trainees ascertained that 'actually seeking work' and 'looking busy' were vital aspects of the demonstration of commitment. This aspect of the professional socialization of accountants has also been noted by Harper (1988). Harper, adopting Goffman's metaphors of 'frontstage' and 'backstage' (1959), described how trainees would "lark around" but would be rebuked for this by more senior staff. Similarly, they would be censured for being seen to be doing 'nothing'. These reprimands are made in order to 'teach' trainees that such behaviour is not appropriate at certain times, i.e. in front of certain audiences. Thus the trainees would learn that backstage behaviour, larking around, is only appropriate when one is with one's peers, away from the gaze of those making judgements about individual's behaviour (i.e. clients and 'superiors' in the firm). The firms need their professionals to know when to behave one way and when to behave in another way:

> "...learning to adopt the role consisted of an ability to discriminate between the audiences before whom it was important to look busy and those in front of whom it did not matter" (Harper, 1988, p.3).

Being able to control one's behaviour in such a way is vital as, from the clients point of view:

> "...part of trusting auditors was dependent on what could be assessed by judging them as people, and therefore the audit firm socialized its personnel to adopt the kind of role that would appear trustworthy: that is, professional" (Harper, 1988, p.7).

Indeed Harper observed that seniors began to show signs of frontstage behaviour in what were essentially backstage environments.

The perceived importance of client judgements of professionalism means that the physical appearance of the trainee accountant also comes under scrutiny. Coffey noted that:

"The firm saw clothing and appearance as vital in displaying and reinforcing a culture which relied upon clients seeing members of the organization as reliable, sensible and 'credible'" (Coffey, 1993, p.186).

Consequently in the early days of their experience in the office and on training courses this aspect of professional life was salient. On one occasion four of the male trainees were made to stand up: one was ridiculed for his white socks, one for his brown shoes, and the other two for having the same suit. The women had to attend a 'secret' session on personal appearance where clothes, make-up, skin care, and hair were discussed. This particular focus on the 'making-up' of accountants and other aspects of personal appearance was absorbed by the trainees and was to become central to their identity as a group, as a member of Western Ridge. This was revealed in a series of sketches performed by the students at the end of the introductory training:

"Feelings were summarized by Alex, one of the students. He said 'if you're smelly you can't be one of us...but Chapmans (another firm) may have you'" (Coffey, 1993, p.201).

Wearing the standard business 'uniform' was also extended to all trainees receiving the same style briefcase from the firm, which bore the firm logo, and which was to be carried on all Western Ridge business; even signatures were subject to the rules of professional appearance.

The role of time-management in Western Ridge was also significant. Coffey's trainees not only received a briefcase from the firm but also a 'filofax'. This personal organizer was described by a trainer as the key to "good organization, good planning, time management and a successful career with Western Ridge" (Coffey, 1994, p.945). Equally important, how one manages one's time can be seen as indicative of one's commitment to the employing organization. That is, the more of your 'own' time that you give up to spend on/at work the more committed you are (e.g. Kanter, 1972). The trainees likewise were soon instructed that they should get used to working weekends and evenings as it was 'part of the job' and were consequently instructed on matters of access to and security of the building in their first week. They were also not able to charge for their overtime until they had accumulated seventy-five hours of overtime which could be taken as leave for examination study, these seventy-five hours were known as 'toil'. In her 1994 paper Coffey argued:

"The graduate accountants recognized the firm's goal of securing both their 'public' and 'private' time. While resenting this they took on board the perceived importance of demonstrating keenness, busyness and commitment to one's work and to Western Ridge" (Coffey, 1994, p.954).

However the disillusionment reported in Coffey's work suggested that the demands for such commitment must be balanced by met expectations on the part of the firm. Whilst trainees may engage in demonstrating appropriate appearance and time-management skills during their training contract it does not follow that this reflects a mutual experience of met expectations. Whether trainees experiencing disappointment in a specific firm choose to stay on and qualify or stay within the profession after qualifying might depend on how they perceive other opportunities within the profession.

Summary

Accountancy in the UK is characterised by several institutional and organizational features:

- Professional socialization of accountants takes place within the context of an institutional fragmentation of professional bodies, a wider cultural recognition of accountancy qualification as a general management credential, and a variety of functions performed by accountants and audit firms.

The study of professionalization has moved towards the study of modes of conduct that are deemed to make up the professional person:

- Demonstration of 'appropriate' ways of being is central to the social closure which is characteristic of the professions, and the jurisdictional work which creates and maintains the position of the professions.
- Creation and maintenance of appropriate professional behaviour (i.e. socialization) begins in earnest, for those wishing to join a profession, when they begin their professional training. Professional training takes place within an organizational context. This organizational context impacts on the nature of individual professionals, that is, on their values and their behaviour.
- Symbolic Interactionist studies have highlighted the socially negotiated nature of experience. The training/induction experiences of trainee professionals are filtered through the expectations, values and

characteristics which accompany the trainee into the new professional training environment.

- There has been little study of the socialization of accountants. However the research that has been conducted suggests that self-presentation to clients and fellow professionals is certainly central to the success of the accountancy profession, and its individual members.

Our purpose in this chapter is not to engage in a wholesale judgement or conclusion on these issues. Rather it is to link the three theses that we have outlined and examined in our research to the theoretical approaches and empirical studies of professionalization that exist. Moreover we have outlined the main features of the wider social context of accountancy to delineate the complexities of the social space in which the subjective identity of 'being a professional' has to operate and contribute to an understanding of how trainee accountants are socialized, either into the 'profession' or other subjective identities.

3 Research Methodology and Methods

Introduction

Given the aims already outlined in Chapters 1 and 2, it was necessary to make particular decisions concerning appropriate research methods. These in turn were partly predicated upon our more general orientations as regards methodology. In this chapter, our objective is to elaborate the methodological stance of the project. Our starting point is a brief outline of general considerations in regard to methodology. More particularly, we outline the tradition of qualitative study in social science research. We then proceed to explain the nature of the research methods used. The chapter then examines specific details of the research project, principally in relation to the semi-structured interview programme which was the main device employed. A final section outlines the role of Computer Aided Qualitative Data Analysis (CAQDAS) in our study. We explain the nature, potentials and difficulties of CAQDAS and give a detailed account of the manner in which it was used in this particular project.

1. General Methodologies

1.1 Positivism and Phenomenology

Social science research, including the study of management, work and organizations, has been disposed to polarize around two broad traditions, those of positivistic and phenomenological research (Easterby-Smith and Thorpe, 1990; Silverman, 1993; Cassell and Symon, 1994). Whilst these broad terms tend to conceal the diversity of social science methodologies (Silverman, 1993), they remain helpful in that they gesture towards the significant philosophical and theoretical issues which properly underlie methodological discussions (Ackroyd, 1996). These considerations are largely occluded if methodology is apprehended in terms of the quantitative-qualitative distinction which is sometimes used as a proxy for that of positivism-phenomenology. For, although it may be generally true that positivism often entails the use of quantitative methods and phenomenology the use of qualitative methods, these are prevailing, although by no means necessary, 'second-order' outcomes of more fundamental issues. These need to be understood, at least in outline.

The positivist view of social science research is complex in that it is varied. Halfpenny (1982), for example, has claimed to identify at least twelve types of positivism. But one widely acceptable understanding would be that of Giddens (1974), who identifies positivism as the view that the concepts and methods of the natural sciences (e.g. in terms of experimentation, observation and the generation of general laws) are the most (or exclusively) appropriate for studying human activity. This view is also disposed to lead on to attempts to specify causal relationships between dependent variables by means of statistical inference. Although positivism has dominated social scientific research (even the term 'social science' pays homage to this), it encounters several fundamental problems. These we outline briefly in order to explain why it has not been considered an appropriate methodology nor, indeed, a *feasible* methodology in any context.

First, in studying social phenomena, causation is readily conflated with correlation. Second, and crucially, social phenomena involve people who are not simply the objects of study but are also active *subjects*. This implies that the fact of being researched can alter behaviour, for example. It also means that the scope for 'scientific' prediction of behaviour is much more limited than in natural science: individuals are likely to alter their behaviour in the light of knowledge and predictions made about them - the explanation often offered for the failure of economic policy and forecasting. As Giddens has outlined this has profound implications for those who suggest that research should be strive to have 'practical' applications in terms of definite solutions to problems:

> "The formulation of critical theory is not an option; theories and findings in the social sciences are likely to have practical (and political) consequences regardless of whether or not the sociological observer or policy-maker decides that they can be 'applied' to a given practical issue" (Giddens, 1984, p.284).

In any case, modern understandings of natural science, especially those informed by quantum physics, suggest that physical phenomena are not independent of the observations made of them, most famously in the case of particle-wave duality. Such developments suggest that the 'way things are' may be an effect of the devices which are used to 'observe reality' and the concepts which are applied to describe it. Moreover, social research into the practices of 'doing science' offer very different accounts of knowledge production from the positivist methodology of the natural sciences (Latour, 1987).

Leaving aside the methodological problems of natural science, the certainty that people are both the subjects of action as well as the objects of enquiry also points to the central importance of interpretation in any study of social behaviour. Winch (1958) gives the classic example of people stopping their cars at red traffic lights. He suggested that a Martian, 'observing' this in positivist fashion, would infer a causal relationship: a red light causes cars to stop. What this knowledge-claim would plainly miss is the crucial importance of the interpretative acts of the driver and, most especially, the interpretation of social rules (traffic regulations) within which the driver, as a social being, assumes an understanding of the correct way to behave at a red light. One way of apprehending this distinction is that the Martian would have great difficulty in understanding someone 'jumping' the lights by deciding to disobey the rules i.e. by acting as a subject and not simply as the object of general laws.

The proposition that human behaviour has to be analyzed in terms of the interpretative acts performed by human beings within a framework of social rules is at the heart of interpretative understandings of social science (Berger and Luckmann, 1966). Although by no means unproblematic, these suggest that human behaviour can only be fully understood by reference to the meanings that behaviours hold for the individuals concerned. One danger with this approach is that it too readily slides into individualism which recognises only the subjective motivations of 'actors'. This is often considered to be the opposite pole of the extreme positivist positions in which human behaviour is asserted to be governed by external and objective laws. But more sophisticated versions of interpretative research methodology seek, as already suggested, to grasp human behaviour in terms of individual action in its social context, and social context in terms of its reproduction through individual action. For these reasons we outlined many of the key features of the accounting profession in the UK in the previous chapter: these form an important historical and institutional context to the process of trainee socialization and we relate them to the findings of our study of trainees in the final chapter.

The issue of the relationship between individual 'action' and social 'structure' has provoked long-standing debate within the social sciences (Giddens, 1979; 1984). Without rehearsing such debates, it is fair to state that most of the major developments in modern sociological theory have been concerned with mediating or subverting the action-structure dichotomy (examples include Giddens' structuration theory, Elias' figurational sociology and Foucault's work on discursive practices and the subject) by recognising in some form the idea that social structure is both the medium and outcome of the actions of individuals. This idea is perhaps most famously known by the expression Giddens (1984) developed for it: the duality of structure.

1.2 Research Methodologies and Research Methods

If research is to be aimed at understanding human actions in their social context in terms of the meanings that such actions hold for individual subjects, certain consequences for the research process are entailed. The most obvious of these is that it is necessary to seek to access the meanings and interpretations which people carry around 'in their heads'. In other words, it is necessary not just to observe what people do, but to strive to gain an understanding of what they think they are doing and why: how and in what terms the subjects of research rationalise their conduct and beliefs and construct their 'social world'. In this sense, as suggested earlier, there appears to be a linkage between a phenomenological or interpretative approach to methodology and a qualitative approach to research method: "qualitative techniques emerge from the phenomenological and interpretative paradigms" (Cassell and Symon, 1994, p.2).

Yet such a linkage is by no means essential. Although some researchers seek simplistically to tie, for example, 'case study' methods to particular methodological positions, there are many researchers employing qualitative methods in pursuit of essentially positivist methodologies (Silverman, 1985; 1993). For example, Bryman and Burgess (1994) adopt an approach to qualitative research in which it is largely treated as a technique which yields complementary yet essentially similar outcomes to quantitative methods. A slightly different view is found in Miles and Hubermann (1994) for whom qualitative research methods are to preferred to quantitative methods in social science because they yield superior information. In both cases, however, there are underlying epistemological and ontological commitments which entail that research method is a means of accessing externally existing reality - reality which is held to exist independently of the interpretations of researchers and the researched. Such approaches are qualitative without being phenomenological except in relatively 'weak' ways, and they are often signalled (albeit not entailed) by the invocation of the concept of 'data' which stands proxy for a methodological position in which reality is 'out there' waiting to be discovered and collected as data. Interpretative approaches stress the senses in which 'data' are produced and constituted through collective knowledge structures rather than existing independently of such structures. Given that 'research' is both a condition and a consequence of knowledge structures, it follows that the research process is not a neutral reading-off of pre-existing data. Rather, 'data' is in some ways an artefact of the research process itself.

How does this discussion translate into attempts to understand the meaning and interpretation of human action in its social context? Consider the example of research aimed at understanding employees' satisfaction at work. The most basic positivist method would be that of 'simple' or 'direct' observation. Yet, unless it is assumed that job satisfaction is manifest through smiling faces and cheerful gestures, this method has very distinct limitations. And if we add to these limitations the certitude that the subjects of the research are likely to know that they are being observed, and are likely to act differently as a result, it can be seen that this 'method' has little to commend it. In relation to the problem of identifying and understanding emerging concepts of professional identity, it is not clear how observation could, in itself, yield substantial and non-trivial knowledge.

A superficially more promising approach would be a survey based method. Here research subjects would be asked to respond to a set of fixed questions, either face-to-face by a surveyor, or in the form of a written questionnaire. Such methods are commonly used in research on organizations, but difficulties attach to this method, particularly where closed surveys are used (that is, where responses must be selected from a specified list). For example, it is very common in survey research to invite respondents to indicate on a five point scale the strength of their agreement or disagreement with a particular proposition (e.g. "I enjoy auditing"). The problems with responses thus gathered include the fact that two respondents answering, say, 'strongly agree' may mean altogether different things by 'strongly'. Similarly, they may interpret the question in quite different ways. One respondent may strongly agree because of the challenge of the job, another because he or she likes the view from the window. Additionally, respondents may deliberately lie or may misunderstand questions. Although the survey method may offer some advantage over trying to find out if people enjoy their work by just watching them, it remains at best a superficial way of conducting social research. And this superficiality mirrors in certain respects the more fundamental methodological issues identified earlier: the survey method treats the object of study as existing independently of the research, and tends to impose meaning upon the researched rather than identifying the meanings ascribed by the researched.

A more promising approach, we suggest, is to seek to explore in detail the understandings of research subjects. Methods available here include participant observation and ethnography; one-to-one interviews with varying degrees of 'structure'; group interviews with varying degrees of structure; collection of documentary materials; and action research. Indeed Tesch (1990) identifies over forty different variants of such qualitative research. This is not the place to discuss these alternatives (see Denzin and Lincoln, 1994 for a compendious overview; Dey, 1993 or Silverman, 1985 for a more concise introduction). Whilst each variant has distinct advantages, the various practical constraints of time and research money, the existing expertise of the researchers and the nature of the research sites has led to an emphasis in this study on one-to-one interviewing of a semi-structured type allied with the collection and interpretation of a variety of documentary materials. This has several advantages. It allows research subjects to express themselves in their own words, and it allows the researcher through conversation to establish trust and rapport, and to probe and question in ways which no survey permits. It is a relatively time-consuming and expensive way of doing research, but not so much as for fully ethnographic work, in which the researcher attempts to probe social actions and interactions by 'living with' the research subjects (Hammersley and Atkinson, 1983). This form of ethnographic study also has its own problems in terms of building trust and eliciting considered responses, although experienced and able researchers develop skills and competencies to deal with this.

In conducting research on issues such as professional and organizational socialization, the advantage of this approach is plain. What people understand by 'profession' and 'organization' may vary widely - and, in this case, did vary widely. The experiences which lead individuals to identify with some notion of profession, or organization (or neither, or both) will also differ considerably, and it may well be that these experiences only come to mind because of the probing of the interviewer. Interpretations of the same event - say, induction training - may diverge between people and, crucially, may diverge from those expected or perceived by those running the induction training.

If the fundamental difference between phenomenological or interpretative and positivist approaches is that the former do not accept the 'natural science' model, it follows that the outcomes of research in the two traditions will be different. Phenomenological research does not and is not intended to generate laws, causalities and predictions. Rather it yields interpretative understandings based upon rich, detailed material gathered in a systematic manner. It is sometimes the case that such findings disappoint practitioners who expect, or hope for, unambiguous results which can be immediately applied in practice. Such disappointment is misplaced for two reasons. First, whilst research that allies itself to ideas of positivism may offer the appearance of certainty, its capacity to deliver explanation and prediction is extremely limited, precisely because of its failure to understand the ways in which subjects interpret and react to any attempt to act upon positivistic recommendations. Analysis of political initiatives in the public sector or corporate reforms in the private often demonstrate that the unintended outcomes of such programmes are more significant than the intended effects. The limitations of scientism in gathering knowledge of individuals in society have dogged the attempt to put economics (McCloskey, 1984) and 'people management' on a putative scientific footing (Jackson and Carter, 1995). Thus the claims or pretensions of positivism, for all its immediate attractions to practitioners, may in the long run disappoint more than phenomenology, with its more modest knowledge claims and ambitions. But, in any case, the 'reflective practitioner' (Schon, 1987) is likely to find in the outcomes of phenomenological research a source of insights which can contribute to a much deeper and more sophisticated understanding of practical realities. And as we noted earlier, the findings of social research have consequences; but we doubt such consequences are intended or 'programmable' in the sense that the outcomes suggest 'policies' for human activities to be steered in predetermined ways.

2. The Project: Details of Method

2.1 The Interview Programme

As already indicated, the main research device we used was that of face-to-face interviewing conducted on a one-to-one basis by the researcher. A total of 77 interviews were conducted across the two Big Six firms studied ('Firm A' and 'Firm B'). We believe that this constitutes the most detailed qualitative research project into the socialization of trainee accountants ever conducted in the UK. The interview programme was informed and developed against the background of other information including previous research experience and discussion with relevant staff in the firms studied. These allowed the refinement of an interview schedule. This schedule varied between interviews in a number of ways. First, as between Firm A and Firm B different structures and processes within the organizations inevitably required different questions to be asked. Equally, the schedule reflected the different stages the research subjects had reached in their training. Finally, there was a degree of variability in that the interviewer pursued issues emerging from research subjects' accounts. This is to be expected as such flexibility is one of the key advantages of the semi-structured interview approach. With these caveats, the interview schedule covered the following core areas:

- Education
- Career/ Career Choice
- Recruitment
- Early Experience of work
- Nature of Division
- In House Training
- External Training
- Examinations
- Nature of Work
- Informal aspects of Work
- Attitude to Firm and Profession

Each interview was conducted over a period of approximately one hour, although this again varied according to the responses given. Interviews were held in private rooms within the buildings of Firms A and B, and were tape-recorded (see section 2.3). These tape-recordings were transcribed prior to coding and analysis (see section 2.4).

2.1.1 Firm A The regional office which we studied is one of the firm's largest UK offices. The office was founded in 1977 and is situated in the financial sector of the city centre. At the time the research began, the firm occupied three floors of a building it shares with other companies and a second building close by which housed the Insolvency Division. Towards the end of the research the Insolvency Division moved into the main building and their premises were no longer used. Space in another building close by was acquired and many of the support functions moved to these premises.

During the period of the research project, approximately 300 professional staff worked at this office, of whom some 80 were on training contracts. Whilst the firm has a number of functional divisions, only three are relevant to trainees, namely Audit, Tax and Insolvency. Each of these divisions directly recruits graduates as trainees for whom ICAEW training and examination is mandatory.

Within each division there is a similar grading structure comprising in outline:

- Partner
- Manager

- Experienced Seniors (qualified)
- Year 3: Senior
- Year 2: Experienced Assistant
- Year 1: Assistant

Trainees are confined to the first three years of this structure. The firm operates (or rather claims to: see Chapter 5) an 'up or out' policy which typically obtains at all grades. For trainees, yearly promotion is strongly linked with progress in professional examinations. After qualification, one consequence of this promotion structure is that there are no 'career seniors' and consequently the structure of divisions is a distinct 'pyramid'. The exact proportions of the pyramid vary across divisions, with audit having proportionally the most trainees.

The programme of interviews was structured to reflect the composition of the trainees both across divisions and across years. This was for two reasons. First, one of the key research questions concerned possible differences in professional socialization across divisions. Second, in that socialization processes operate over time, and training is envisaged as a progression, it was obviously necessary to have representation of all trainee grades in the interview programme. It was decided to select approximately half of all of the trainees for interviewing, this figure being compatible with the desire to achieve a broad coverage whilst meeting cost and time constraints. Within each division and year group, selection of trainees was on a random basis. The composition of the interview programme by year and division was as follows:

Table 1 Firm A Interview Programme

	Audit	Tax	Insolvency	Total
Year 1	8 (2)	5 (2)	1 (0)	14 (4)
Year 2	8 (2)	2 (2)	2 (0)	12 (4)
Year 3	6 (1)	3 (2)	2 (1)	11 (4)
Total	22 (5)	10 (6)	5 (1)	37 (12)

Numbers in ( ) indicate the number of trainees interviewed in that category that are female.

2.1.2 Firm B The office which we studied dates back to 1875 and is the head office within its region. Consequently it is one of the firm's largest UK offices. It is situated in the financial sector of the city centre, and is the sole occupier of a six floor building. During the period of the research, there were approximately 240 professional staff of whom 86 were trainees, predominantly located within audit functions.

Of the various functional divisions, the two relevant to the study were Audit and Tax. Both divisions are further sub-divided into departments based on client type. There are 4 audit departments and 3 corporate tax departments plus 3 specialist tax departments. The divisions are hierarchically organized as follows:

Audit

- Partner
- Senior Manager
- Manager 1
- Manager
- Assistant Manager
- Supervisor
- Senior
- Assistant 1
- Assistant 2
- Assistant 3

Tax

- Partner
- Senior Manager
- Manager 1
- Managers
- CTS1, PTS1
- CTS2, PTS2
- CTA1, PTA1
- CTA2, PTA2
- CTA3, PTA3

(CT= Corporate Tax. PT = Personal Tax)

There is no explicit 'up or out' policy in Firm B, although it would seem untypical for individuals to remain for long periods without achieving promotion. Graduates wishing to train as chartered accountants will generally join the Audit division as taking the ICAEW exams is mandatory for those joining this division. The majority of graduates joining the Tax division take the ATT and the ATTI exams, however, a small number are ICAEW students.

The interview programme was concerned with ICAEW trainees and, therefore, was skewed towards the Audit division where such trainees are concentrated. As with Firm A, the programme covered all years of training and was based upon a random sample of approximately 50% of the trainees. The breakdown of the interviewees was as follows:

Table 2   Firm B Interview Programme

	Audit	*Tax*	*Total*
Year 1	9 (2)	3 (1)	12 (3)
Year 2	13 (4)	2 (1)	15 (5)
Year 3	12 (5)	1 (0)	13 (5)
Total	34 (11)	6 (2)	40 (13)

Numbers in ( ) indicate the number of trainees interviewed in that category that are female.

2.2 Other Research Methods

Although the interview programme was the principal research instrument employed, the project did utilise other sources of material. First, inevitably, the background knowledge of the research team was a natural source of understandings and interpretations. Second, in the course of the research a considerable amount of time was spent on the premises of Firms A and B, a form of research sometimes designated 'hanging around and listening in' (Strauss, 1987). This can form a useful counterpart to more formal methods for providing a richer sense of the research site. Included in this category would be a range of formal and informal contacts with members of each firm during the course of the research.

A perhaps more substantial source of research material came in the form of documents and brochures supplied by the firms. These helped to assemble a background for the interviews by helping to explain the kinds of 'messages' which trainees might be expected to have received and which would therefore be directly relevant to the socialization process. For example, graduate recruitment material was one kind of documentary source which seemed to be vital in shaping trainees' early perceptions of the organization and of the type of work that they would be undertaking. Similarly, documentary material on appraisal and evaluation was vital to the formulation of relevant and detailed questioning of trainees about their experience of these matters. Clearly it would not be an effective use of interview time to require each trainee to repeat the basic details of such procedures.

2.3 Ethical Issues

We took seriously the ethical issues posed by research of this type (Lee, 1993). This concern was not only for reasons of moral scruple but also of pragmatism. It was central to the successful accumulation of material that the firms and individuals involved would provide us with frank and sincere responses to questions. Often these questions would relate to quite sensitive issues. The attitude of a junior member of a large firm to his or her employer or profession might be a matter the individual would prefer to conceal. It was recognised not only that all of the individuals had an absolute right to confidentiality but also that, were this right not to be respected, it was likely that future interviewees would learn of this and be less than forthcoming as a result. It was therefore a cardinal principle of the research that no information about individuals would be fed back either informally or formally to anyone else within the firm or outside the firm.

By the same token information about the firms was never divulged outside the research team. In this book, as mentioned elsewhere, we have concealed or even distorted information which could be regarded as sensitive to the firms in the study. Moreover, our prior knowledge and experience of Big Six firms led us to expect that they see themselves as 'sensitive' organizations and this was certainly our experience in this study. However, it was not in the nature of the research that commercially sensitive material was gathered, and no information relating to clients was relevant. Therefore, in practice most of the ethical issues posed by the research applied more to individuals than to firms.

In recognition of this, elaborate care was taken to secure the consent of individuals to tape-recording of interviews following a full explanation of the uses to which material would be put and guarantees of confidentiality. Where permission was not granted (this happened in just two cases) a written note of the interview was kept. Interviewees were then assigned a code which protected their identity whilst allowing us to categorise the interview by firm, division, year and gender. The interview tape bearing only this code was transcribed by a professional transcriber who was entirely independent of the firms studied and of the university. Tapes and transcripts were sent by recorded delivery post.

Transcripts never carried the names of individuals and, on receipt, were entered into a software package for qualitative data analysis. In the next section we elaborate our use of the computer 'code and retrieval' analysis software.

2.4 Computer Aided Qualitative Data Analysis (CAQDAS)

Computer Aided Qualitative Data Analysis (CAQDAS) has in recent years become widely used and accepted within social science and organizational research (Fielding and Lee, 1991; Kelle, 1995; Richards and Richards, 1994). There are a number of software packages for managing and analyzing qualitative research material now available, and several reference works outlining their various features, strengths and weaknesses (Tesch, 1990; 1991; Seidel *et al*, 1995; Weitzman and Miles, 1995). Whilst the field is subject to rapid change due both to technical change and emerging methodological discussion, one of the most popular software packages available is *The Ethnograph* (Seidel, 1988) which has been described as 'the application of choice for many contemporary researchers and research groups' (Weaver and Atkinson, 1994, p. 4). This choice may partly reflect issues of cost. With rival packages such as 'Metamorph' costing in the region of £1,000 (Catterall and Maclaren, 1996), The Ethnograph is relatively cheap. In addition, the former programme is reported as being poor for coding purposes (Catterall and Maclaren, 1996) whereas Weaver and Atkinson (1994) regard coding as one of *The Ethnograph's* strengths.

Coding is at the heart of CAQDAS, although, as will shortly be discussed, the analysis of material should not be reduced simply to coding (Lee and Fielding, 1996; cf. Coffey *et al*, 1996). In essence *The Ethnograph* allows interview material to be coded line-by-line under categories determined by the researcher. The process commences with the computer generation of a line numbered transcript. These were on average some 2000 lines in length, representing around 30 pages of text for each interview conducted (the research project as a whole therefore generated around 160,000 lines of transcription). This line-numbered transcript is the raw material for coding. Each line can be assigned up to twelve codes from the code set devised by the researchers, although it would be possible to assign twice that number simply by inputting the same interview into the software twice. In practice it is unnecessary to code every line individually: rather, blocks of text can be coded under as many codes as are appropriate subject to the limitation that a maximum of seven overlaps is possible between blocks of text. By the same token, some lines or blocks of text may be deemed as unworthy of coding if they supply material which is unoriginal, irrelevant or uninteresting.

On completion of the coding of transcripts, the coded interview can be entered into *The Ethnograph* package so that the entire interview programme becomes a database. This can the be searched by codeword (or by a combination of codewords) and is thereby a powerful *data management* tool. Moreover, details of the age, position, division, gender, firm etc. of an interviewee are input onto an initial 'front sheet' for each coded interview which allows the researcher to target more specific searches of significant sub-samples of the interviewee population in relation to particular research issues, e.g. searches by gender and position within an audit firm.

There are two major issues which affect the use and value of the package. One is the initial decision of which codes should be used. The second is the interpretation of the interview material in order to allocate codes.

2.4.1 The Codes The allocation of codes to the material is by no means a straightforward process and, indeed, is fraught with methodological and theoretical pitfalls. Perhaps the central aspect of the problem is that 'codes are not inherent in the data; rather they are inherent to the interpretation of the data' (Weaver and Atkinson, 1994, p.66). Since our general methodological position outlined earlier does not allow that social reality exists independently of the interpretations of researchers and researched, so it would be inconsistent to assume that the transcribed interviews could give rise to appropriate codes. Rather, the process of code formation is one in which meaning and order are imposed upon the material which it does not inherently possess. This is of course true regardless of whether CAQDAS is used, but CAQDAS does pose particular difficulties. If codes are drawn up in advance of their application they will tend to be imposed upon data, perhaps in inappropriate ways. There is, then, a tendency both to rigidify and even to deify the interpretations embodied within the codes. However, in the same way that certain styles of ethnographic research adopt a 'grounded' approach to theory formation and development (Glaser and Strauss, 1967), the development of coding does not necessarily reflect the simple imposition of pre-defined ideas and concepts independent of the data. In our study the elaboration of the codes was not undertaken until a substantial number of interviews had already been conducted and discussed within the research team.

Nevertheless, recognising the power of coding to embody meaning and thereby to impose meaning leads to consideration of a number of more specific problems in code construction (and application):

What is the appropriate level of generality?
A very general code suffers from its lack of power to 'cut' the data. For example, in this project, a code like 'working in an accounting firm' would probably be applicable to every line of the transcript. On the other hand, a code like 'St. Andrew's University' might apply to only one line in the whole set of transcripts.

What is the appropriate level of dynamism?
A set of codes which is 'static' is one drawn up at the outset of the research and never altered. A more 'dynamic' set is modified in line with emerging issues. The static approach suffers from an obvious inflexibility, but too dynamic approach might lead to a never-ending process of coding and re-coding data.

What is the source of the codes?
Codes can be drawn up from three obvious sources: existing research questions, theory, 'data', but also and more importantly the interaction of these three elements during the conduct of the research. Whilst the idea of 'data' as a source may seem to contradict the epistemological commitments of our methodological approach this is not so, since it is recognised that the researched are actors in reality-construction. Therefore, researchers cannot ignore persistent meanings and interpretations and these can provide a source of codes. In any case, even where the 'data' does not yield codes directly, it is likely to influence the extent to which codes are actually used. The other sources of codes are more straightforward. Clearly, in the present project, concern with professional and organizational socialization yielded certain self-evident codes which derived from the basic research questions outlined at the outset of this book. Finally, theory, in that it is itself a way in which data is structured and called into existence will be relevant in coding: the main issue here, as already indicated, is to recognise the theory-ladenness of coding rather than to see it as a purely 'technical' activity.

Bearing these issues in mind, as stated above the identification of appropriate codes was not attempted until several interviews had been completed. The intention was to identify from the issues emerging in the interview what the categories for coding should be, rather than to conduct interviews around the categories. This was a way of addressing the aforementioned issue of dynamism. By waiting before constructing codes, it was felt that there was a better chance of avoiding the need for excessive change, and, in practice, this seemed to work well: few modifications were made to the codes after the initial piloting.

This pilot process involved drawing up an initial list of 34 codes. The codes chosen were substantially driven by the substantive research questions of the project. These questions gave rise to a number of fairly obvious codes such as PROF, PROFKNOW, CULORGID and OTHERDIVS (see below for meanings). Other codes were more theoretically generated, for examples HIERCON and RESIST. As regards the issue of generality, it was decided to opt for varying degrees of specificity and to subdivide large issues such as training (which had six separate codings including a residual or catch-all code).

Having drawn up this initial list, each member of the research team first coded the *same* interview. A meeting was held subsequently in which the categories were discussed, refined, dropped or added according to the difficulties experienced in operationalizing the categories or according to their failure to yield adequate coding for interview material. Subsequently, changes were kept to a minimum, although new codes were introduced afterwards but these were mainly made during the early stages of coding in order to avoid substantial re-coding of interviews already processed.

This process yielded a final list of 36 categories which, with their abbreviations for coding, was as follows:

- RECSEL: Recruitment and selection processes
- EARLYEXP: Early experience of firm/profession
- CAREER: Career (plans, expectations etc.)
- SOCIALTIME: Socializing and time or time-keeping issues
- COOPCOMP: Co-operation and competition within and between firms
- TRPROF: Professional training including external tutoring
- TRMODE: Training mode (full time, link, split-intensive, end-loaded)
- TRINHOUSE: In-house training
- TRMENTOR: Mentors and mentoring
- TRGEN: Training - general/other
- APPFORM: Formal appraisal procedures
- APPINFORM: Informal appraisal
- APPGEN: Appraisal - general/ other
- PERSON: References to inter-personal relations and personality (own or others including clashes of personality)
- ATROCITY: Atrocity stories (organizational narratives or experiences, not necessarily bad; cf. Silverman, 1993)
- HIERCON: Hierarchy and control processes within firms
- RESIST: Resistance to forms of organizational control
- EMP: Empathy (e.g. between staff)
- LUCK: Luck (e.g. role in career)
- GENDER: References to perceived gender roles, discrimination in work and study
- SUCFAIL: Accounts of or references to organizational or career success and failure
- REWARDS: Reward systems within firms: formal/informal
- PROF: References to profession and professional
- PROFKNOW: Professional knowledge and expertise
- CLIENTS: Clients of firms
- OTHERDIVS: Perceptions of other divisions
- OTHERFIRM: Comments about or attitudes expressed towards other accountancy firms

- SELFIMAGE: Self-image of interviewee
- CULORGID: Culture (organizationally specific practices or identities)
- CULFITIN: Processes of adjustment; Fitting in to an organization's culture
- CULLANG: Culturally specific language or discourses
- CULOBSDRS: Culture (Objects and Dress)
- EXPGOOD: Good experience
- EXPBAD: Bad experience
- PROGRESS: Reference to changes over time
- GOLD: Very interesting or important comment; could be about anything

It will be clear that these categories allow for a certain degree of overlap and that they offer the opportunity for interesting conjunctions to emerge between, for example, professional and organizational issues. The overriding advantage is of course the speed with which very lengthy data can be searched for relevant material.

2.4.2 The Coding Process Having identified the codes to be used is only the beginning of the complexities encountered in undertaking CAQDAS. The application of codes is also a process requiring careful thought. The main issues here are the judgement of the meaning of codes and the interpretation of the text to be coded, and the extent of segmenting to establish context. To illustrate the difficulties here, a short piece of transcribed text from the research will be used:

```
601     'I think it's because the whole reason why we have to do split …
602     I think very much was because it fitted with audit in the audit
603     busy season,  they needed auditors back in for those three months
604     which doesn't necessarily fit with tax but we haven't got as
605     much of a busy season so I think they probably did lose out a
606     bit there.  Our chaps' results were always a bit higher because
607     we had more time in the office and could get home to work in
608     the evenings.'
```

Here the interviewee is comparing the experience of being a tax trainee with that of an audit trainee. The most obvious code to use is OTHERDIVS. The question of segmenting is difficult in this case. Line 606 on its own might be sufficient for some purposes, but when retrieved it would be very hard to make sense of on its own. Any choice on segmenting might possibly cut out some relevant contextual material. But there is more going on within this segment than a comment about other divisions. There is also reference to the split intensive mode of training, warranting a TRMODE code and to the difficulties of professional training (TRPROF). The segment also suggests the different time patterns for trainees and their potential significance and could be coded SOCIALTIME as well. The explanation of possible reasons for success and failure in exams might suggest a SUCFAIL coding. It might even be argued that the slightly cynical implication of the lines 601-603 tells us something about organizational culture and could be coded CULORGID (although whether the reason for such a coding would be self-evident on retrieval is unclear). The reference to 'chaps' on 606 could imply using the GENDER code, but such a usage might possibly lead to a swamping of low-level gender information on retrieval, depending upon the degree of importance the concept has in the research problematic. In addition, the usage might be part of a culturally specific language (CULLANG).

Just from this short analysis it is possible to see that the ascription of codes to data is not self-evident and cannot be assumed to be dictated by the data (despite the claims of grounded theory). Moreover, the decisions made at the stage of coding will strongly influence the shape and nature of the eventual analysis. These difficulties are compounded when several people are involved in coding. In the research, these difficulties were addressed in two ways. First, the initial and indeed lengthy meeting to refine codes was also used to compare in detail how the codes had been used. Through this discussion, a degree of common understanding was generated as to how the codes should be used. Secondly, whilst all the project team were engaged in coding, the actual entry of the codes onto computer was only performed by one researcher who was thereby able to operate a final check for comparability of coding.

Having established a database of coded transcripts, it is possible to commence analysis of the material. Perhaps the major misconception that persists around CAQDAS is the assumption that the coding somehow constitutes analysis (Weaver and Atkinson, 1994; Kelle, 1995). The crudest manifestation of such a view would be simply to assign significance to a code based upon the number of its usage, ignoring, for example, variations in these usages. In this research, little analytical usage was made of The Ethnograph codings on their own terms. The package was used primarily as an organizing and searching device to pull out material relating to the main lines of analysis. Of course, in searching out material, it is inevitable and desirable that new lines of enquiry will be suggested - that the researchers could compare accounts given by interview subjects and think about the material in new ways - but this represents only a gently analytical approach to CAQDAS.

Conclusion

In this chapter we have:

- identifed our methodological position as being rooted in a phenomenological approach to social science rather than in a positivist approach;
- Discussed the different research methods and indicated our choice amongst these;
- provided an outline of the interview programme on which the analysis in the remainder of this book is based;
- summarised the characteristics of the regional offices of the two firms which served as research sites for our study; and
- explained the use of CAQDAS in assisting in the research process.

4 The Processes of Socialization

Introduction

The first thesis which we set out to explore was:

> *Socialization processes focus not only upon examination performance, but presentation to clients and ability to integrate with the social norms of peers, managers and partners.*

In this chapter we examine trainee experience with a view to highlighting the various elements of 'successful' performance with which trainees identify and are expected to develop whilst on a training contract at the two offices that are our research sites. Clearly, passing the professional examinations is a necessary condition of membership of the profession, but trainees are also judged on a variety of other behaviours and achievements whilst training. Failure to gain an understanding of and to enact any of these other requirements can jeopardise the 'career progression' of the trainee in the firm and consequently affects their chances of successfully completing the training contract, and entering the profession. In this chapter we identify and elaborate the nature of these other social and cultural norms, highlight the processes through which trainees become aware of these, and describe how they are assessed on their 'performance'. That is, we explore the socialization of trainee accountants at our research sites. Whilst this analysis details the obligatory behaviours and attitudes required for a trainee accountant to complete successfully the training contract in our research sites, it also begins to document the development of values and behaviours that trainees identify with being professional, although a detailed analysis of the professional identity of the trainees is considered in Chapter 5.

The starting points for any analysis of organizational socialization are the formal systems for recruiting, training and appraising trainees. Other aspects of the trainees' experience (such as daily contact with colleagues, and early contact with clients) also impact on their socialization. This chapter examines both the role of these formal systems and the nature and form of informal socialization processes with regard to trainees learning how to 'regulate the self'. Within this analysis the significance of presentation to clients, and the social norms of colleagues assume a prominent role.

1. Formal Systems of Socialization

1.1 Recruitment and Selection

Recruitment can be seen as the first stage of the socialization process in that by selecting certain people the firm, or personnel department within the firm, is attempting to introduce types of skills and behaviours that are seen as desirable. There are various elements to reducing the pool of potential applicants to the firm, starting with the recruitment document. The recruitment brochures of both Firm A and Firm B present a literal image of the trainee as a high-flyer, a 'jet-setting' business advisor. The brochures are high quality, glossy and colourful, and give an impression of financial success on the part of the firm. Firm B breaks the main text of its 1997 brochure with references to the prominent organizations that are its clients, and both firms' brochures have references to "international prospects", and quotations from current trainees. The following quotation specifically focuses on business advice as a core aspect of the firm's identity:

> "Clients respect us as leaders. We are well established in the market place, and seen as one of the best firms for business advice" (Big Six Firm, recruitment brochure, 1997).

Another brochure also identifies the role of its employees in similar terms:

> "We're business advisers in the broadest sense and our clients turn to us on an enormous range of issues" (Big Six Firm, recruitment brochure, 1997).

And in this way the intention is that those persons attracted to this idea of self, looking for a career that has these characteristics, and believing they are the sort of person capable of being successful in such an environment, will apply for interview. The need for technical and social competence is reflected in the descriptions of training the firms present in the recruitment brochures:

> "...you will be given the opportunity to develop business, technical, management and interpersonal skills to fulfil your potential and add significant value to your career, and to our business" (Big Six Firm, recruitment brochure, 1997).

> "What does [the] training package broadly cover:
> Practical experience
> Examination tuition leading to professional qualifications
> Personal and professional development" (Big Six Firm, recruitment brochure, 1997).

As we detail later, however, recruits are not always prepared to see themselves in this way.

Both firms restrict recruitment into their ICAEW training contracts to graduates, although in Firm A we did find a few exceptions to this. Whilst a few graduates that are recruited by these offices may be 'Oxbridge' it seems that the majority of these apply to and are recruited by the London offices of the firms. Both firms considered applications from the 'new universities'. However, in the sample interviewed only one trainee (of 37) at Firm A, and only three (of 40) at Firm B had graduated from such universities. Moreover, both firms have more non-relevant than relevant (i.e. accounting) graduates, which is in line with the general trend of recruiting. Firm A is apparently unusual in having no standard minimum UCAS points level. Their policy is to look at all applicants, with a good degree, as they hold that some people do not prove their ability until degree level. Firm B looks only at application forms from applicants with at least 22 UCAS points.

1.1.1 Social Skills and Norms in Recruitment Processes Having been selected for a first interview, candidates applying to both firms are interviewed and sit a numeracy test. In both firms choice of this type of selection technique seemed to be indicative of the emerging importance of formal Human Resource Management (HRM) techniques in the administration of staff training as well as the importance to the firm of a candidate being adequately numerate. In Firm A the numeracy test had only been recently introduced (1993) whilst it had been in operation for longer at Firm B.

Candidates successful at the first interview stage were asked to return for a second interview and various other assessment exercises at both firms. At Firm A, 1993 also saw the introduction of a written exercise and a 'productive thinking' exercise of the type familiar to practitioners of psychometric testing in occupational psychology. These tests were introduced, according to the rubric of the test paper, to test the ability of candidates with regard to key skills found to be important in successful performance at senior levels of the firm. Despite this encroachment of the influence of formalised means of evaluating potential recruits, good inter-personal skills were viewed as paramount and the results of these tests seen as less important than demonstration of inter-personal skills.

At Firm B candidates were asked to perform an in-tray exercise and a group exercise. A set of 'competencies' had been developed at Firm B that were held to be crucial to the strategic positioning of the firm. These competencies were used as a framework to judge performance during the recruitment stage and to judge performance once trainees are successfully employed by the firm.   Again, despite the apparent emphasis upon recruitment procedures and 'testing', members of the personnel department in Firm B claimed that they occasionally found it difficult to persuade partners that a candidate whom they 'think is the best thing since sliced bread' was not appropriate if he or she had performed badly on the assessment tests. As in Firm A tensions were apparent between the formal mechanisms of administrative and personnel appraisal and the 'feelings' of the experienced practising partners or mangers.   However, as it is seen to be necessary to adhere to test results, it seemed that test scores were generally seen as more important in Firm B than in Firm A.   Nevertheless, it was stressed that if a candidate performed well on the tests but was not liked by the partner (in Firm B) it was highly unlikely that they would be offered a training contract - a clear distinction from the case in Firm A.

Interviews permitted recruiters to assess the social skills (manner and appearance etc.) of applicants.   They were regarded as allowing the opportunity to make some assessment of the 'type' of person, with a view to judging whether he or she will 'fit into' the organization.   At Firm A the applicant, at second interview stage, was invited to meet other members of the firm and was taken to lunch by a trainee.   The idea of matching of 'personalities' was deemed to be important both to the firm and the applicant. Yet despite this attention towards recruitment designed to match psychometric profiles of applicants, trainees often reported that (in the recruitment brochures also) there was little difference between what the Big Six firms seemed to offer.   Consequently their decision to accept an offer often rests on the interview experience in terms of how they felt in the environment that they would be working in, how they got on with the specific people they met or even seemingly trivial details, such as being offered a plate of biscuits with the usual drinks.   This trainee, for example, chose to work for Firm A on the basis of the pleasant experience he had of people during the recruitment process:

> "I didn't enjoy the interview with the 'Otherfirm' chap at all.   He was a bit aggressive.   I don't think he was a Graduate himself and he seemed to have a chip on his shoulder ... Yes, the experience (here) was completely different because all the others sort of lump you together.   I had a second interview with a Bank and there would be ten to twelve people at final interview stage and it was very competitive and everybody tried to do everyone else down and make themselves shine but with Thisfirm it was just so different because it was the candidate on their own so you really felt as though they were having a thorough look at you and you weren't being competitive.   There was a tour of the office and they took you out to lunch and it was very friendly very personal and at the

end of the day I thought 'Yes, I'd like to work here, it's great' (Tax Trainee, 1st Year).

Ironically, 'aggressiveness', far from being an undesirable personal attribute, however, was often viewed in Firm A as a characteristic of the firm's type. Nevertheless, despite the firm rhetoric of psychometric profiling and testing, this 'two-way' selection process assisted the process whereby the people joining the firm were similar in several respects to their peers and their superiors. In this way, the 'firm' can be relatively assured that its new trainees (at least within a work context) would (in accord with their interviewers): dress appropriately (that is, in conservative versions of contemporary business attire, such as, for male trainees, a dark suit and shirt and tie that is stylish rather than garish); be ambitious; work hard; be intellectually competent; be socially skilled and claim an interest in the 'business world'. Despite these sorts of normalising processes there were, of course, always exceptions, not least because such attributes can be always be assumed by the interviewee for the purposes of the interview. One trainee who found the general values of people in the firm a little at odds with their own beliefs commented:

"I personally and it sounds harsh but I would say the social culture is the worst thing. I think, I was personally very glad when the eighties ended. I thought, I still feel we've progressed a lot in the nineties but I get the impression that most Accountants and this isn't just Thisfirm because I've met a lot of other Accountants at the balls and so forth would quite happily bring back Thatcher and hanging in one fell swoop so yes that is the worst thing about it... We are very materialist type of people. The whole culture's about money. You work with money all day and it's about things. The Managers get a car allowance, and the sort of cars they have two seater sports cars..." (Audit Trainee, 1st Year).

Nevertheless, the recruitment process, by focusing not only upon academic ability but also the match between the social norms of recruiters and applicants, shaped the conduct of the trainees as a group by ensuring that, on the whole, those people who fit the 'model' of 'successful employee' that currently existed within the organization joined the firm.

1.1.2 Presentation to the Client in Recruitment As we emphasize at several points in our analysis, the idea of client service highlighted the paramount importance of acceptable social ('business') conduct to the survival and success of the firms. This is stressed at the trainees' earliest contact with the firm, that is, in the recruitment brochures:

"Firm B's position as a world leader in the accountancy profession has been achieved by providing a service of flawless technical excellence....By striving for excellence in everything we do and managing our client relationships at the highest level of professionalism, we have developed a global track record that is hard to beat" (Firm B, recruitment brochure, 1997).

"Our values are why we're here and why we'll be here for a long time to come. They underpin the four cornerstones of our business strategy - to increase market share, to achieve total client satisfaction, to look after our people, and to manage the quality and risk of our assignments" (Firm A, recruitment brochure, 1997).

Of course in general terms at interview trainees are expected to affirm their potential ability to "integrate with the norms of peers, managers and partners"; that is their ability to fit into the organization and operate effectively and, as part of that, to provide the client service that the firm expects. The client not only expects technical service but a certain persona is required, as Dingwall (1976) remarks about health visitors:

"In order to succeed as a student it is centrally important to establish that one is the right sort of person to be a health visitor" (p.337).

Likewise in accountancy: not only are social norms and behaviour important with regard to being accepted in the firm and feeling part of the firm, they are also rationalised in terms that suggest they are also crucial in the performing of technical tasks. This seems to be evidenced in the results of the recent 1996 ICAEW/MORI questionnaire where 81% of members who completed the questionnaire stated that 'Good interpersonal/communication skills' are one of the top five skills a newly qualified accountant should have. So, whilst degree subject and awarding institution may vary, both interviewers and interviewees understand that terms like 'leadership potential' may be signalled by being a sport's team captain by one applicant and a student society treasurer by another, and these types of signifiers are often sufficient enough for firms' interviewers to decide that their new trainees can come into contact with their clients within a few weeks of joining the firm without risking the quality of the work or reputation of the firm. In this way apparently key individual attributes are often 'demonstrated' to the interviewers on the basis of *shared* social interests in such activities as team sports or student societies.

1.2 Performance Appraisal

Formal performance appraisal systems should be expected to be a major tool for shaping the behaviour of trainees as the appraisal forms and competencies are normative procedures. For example, Townley (1994) states:

"In HRM, the process of constituting the subject is evident in orientation, socialization and induction programmes; training; appraisal systems which try to inculcate the correct behavioural norms..." (1994, p.119).

The evidence from our study on the degree to which the 'constitution of subjectivity' (Townley, 1994) can be linked to the formal appraisal procedures is, however, ambiguous. Certainly the presence of HRM techniques such as appraisal and (formal) mentoring seems to be increasing. In both firms trainees have formal mid-year and annual appraisals. In Firm A these are conducted by the trainee's counselling manager and so Institute training records requirements are attended to at the same time as 'performance', as viewed by the firm, is discussed. In Firm B the manager appraisal and counselling partner interviews are separate and so trainees have four appraisal meetings a year.

In each firm the counselling manager/partner is seen as the advocate of their trainees at promotion meetings and so on. However, the degree to which the appraisal process structures progression within the firms is limited. For example, annual progression from one grade to the next is almost a certainty for trainees (providing there are not serious doubts about ability expressed in the formal appraisal documents). There is, however, room for discretion about the salary awarded. Variable pay rises tend to be considered, for the first-time, at the end of the trainees' second year. The records of the firms' formal rating system are used as part of the procedure for deciding on the amount awarded to each trainee although trainees often perceived the appraisal forms to be more ritualistic rather than substantive: salary and promotion prospects were seen more often to be signalled through much less formal relationships and assessments within the firm. Much of this relatively weak exercise of control by the formal appraisal process reflected the "going through the motions" conduct taken towards the forms by appraisers and subsequently by appraisees (cf. Dirsmith *et al*, 1997, p.10) as we elaborate below.

Mid-year and annual appraisals were based on appraisal forms that are completed on a trainee's performance on each audit job that lasts for more than a few days, after three months for tax, and after 'substantial' pieces of work for insolvency trainees. This process involves the trainees completing a section on the appraisal form that relates to their objectives. The trainee in-charge on the job (or manager if it is an in-charge being rated) then completes the evaluation section and passes this onto the manager for signing and comments. This is then passed back to the trainee before being placed in the trainee's file in the Personnel department. In Firm A face-to-face discussion about a job review may take place if either party feels it is necessary, and this generally takes place for everybody after their first few jobs. In Firm B there is not usually a formal face-to-face meeting to discuss the review. The trainees are evaluated on a scale in relation to the following 'categories' (these are paraphrases of the actual qualities listed in each appraisal document):

Firm A
Technical Ability
Standard of Work
Responsibility
People Development (In-Charge Only)
Client Service
Professionalism

Firm B
Client Service: Networking and Professional Attitude
Business Skills: Commercial Skills and Future Business
Management: Task and People Management Skills, and People Development
Effectiveness: Committed to Task, Dependable and Flexible.
Social Skills: Communication Skills, Confidence
Thinking Skills: Systematic Thinking and Proactive Thinking
Professional and Technical Skills

Firm A's list of appraised competencies also encompassed wider aspects of personality such as:

"Defends own view point but is prepared to admit when wrong	or	Is too compliant or lacks flexibility
Possesses justified confidence in own abilities	or	Lacks confidence or confidence exceeds actual ability"

These wider attributes are not explicitly evaluated in the appraisal system of Firm B. This may be indicative of the reported emphasis at Firm A on the ideal of the Firm A type: that is, the belief that people working for this firm are collectively distinctive (see Chapter 5). Thus the 'whole', or at least more of, the person is assessed which allows the appraiser's basic judgements of the appraisee to be expressed and which made the process perhaps more important than in Firm B. The form in Firm A also has a final section asking raters to choose one of five overall ratings which comment on current level of competency and consequent indications for future performance in the firm.

It is claimed in both firms that the competencies rated reflect the firms' views of what behaviour, or what type of person, is necessary for all professional staff to display, or be, if they wish to stay with the firm. The appraisal forms of each firm ask appraisers to judge and record the level of competency the trainee is exhibiting, and by doing so to state whether the trainee is behaving satisfactorily. The structure of the appraisal systems demands a focus on performance that segments aspects of behaviour. However the practice appeared to be that evaluation in these fixed terms was not easily achieved and raters (who might not be qualified themselves) commented that they found it difficult to differentiate between some of the categories or even to 'think' in the terms in which they were asked to appraise a trainee. For example:

"Then the bit on the front where you've got these grids of various skills ... I think everyone finds them a little bit bizarre because it's difficult to categorise within them" (Audit Trainee, 3rd Year).

This trainee, expressing an opinion also held by other trainees, found the segmentation of overall behaviour artificial and somehow not representative of the work that is done or the behaviour that is required and observed. Raters were usually the seniors/in-charges who bear a good deal of responsibility for particular tasks (audit, tax consultation etc.), and they reported that the appraisal system did not make them any more vigilant than they would be otherwise. As part of their accountability they felt that they monitored and formed judgements about the work of their juniors regardless of appraisal responsibilities. In addition, as a result of having gone through the same experiences as those they are appraising they report that they 'know' what the trainees need to be doing. Consequently the formal structuring of this can feel both awkward and an unnecessary elaboration of what appraisers believed they already knew. Consequently appraisal reports reflected more general and, often, prior judgements of the trainee than specific consideration of each listed competency.

From the perspective of trainees, some found the process useful but many had at least some criticism of the systems. The main criticisms of the appraisal systems centred around delayed feedback from job reviews and the subjectivity of the rating procedure, a state that seemed to reflect the ritualistic and critical stance that appraisers took towards the process.

"the only problem is too many times you don't get them back 'til, they just don't come back quick enough...I came back off an examination course last week and found four or five appraisals that I'd got back in my tray but they were for jobs that vary from, they were all from February, March. It's like four or five months later I got them back" (Audit Trainee, 3rd Year).

"when you've got a standard form, which is standard, doesn't change obviously, but you've got a hundred different people filling it in it's not a standard form anymore" (Audit Trainee, 1st Year).

In a way this latter quotation reflects our earlier comments (in Chapter 3) upon the use of survey methods in social research. The trainee questions the meaning that can be attributed to one person rating them 'good' on a particular competency as opposed to another. Differences between appraisers were widely recognised among the appraisees:

"I think generally most of mine have been fair but they just vary so much according to who's doing the evaluation and what qualities they look for in people. They are very subjective" (Audit Trainee, 2nd Year).

Some trainees also commented that the forms 'made' the person completing the rating form look for criticisms and emphasise an 'error' more than is called for:

"He'll say look 'We've raised some points here which need to be followed up because you've not completed it properly' and then you'll say 'Right, OK I'll do that' and it's just one tick mark and he'll put 'Jeremy must remember to consider all his tick marks and review his work' and you think 'Look, there's only one', but that's because there's pressure on them I believe anyway to find errors" (Audit Trainee, 1st Year).

Detailed monitoring is nevertheless demanded of raters as a function of the structure of the appraisal form. Because of this need for a detailed focus comments on the forms are sometimes seen as unduly critical. On the other hand, because of time constraints on raters and/or lack of effort on the part of raters, comments were also sometimes regarded as bland and unhelpful.

Some trainees who have rated others also reported that raters can find completing the assessments difficult because they did not wish to 'upset' another trainee by giving them a bad appraisal.

Whilst one might expect the competencies on the appraisal forms to be a major tool for shaping the behaviour of trainees, there was little evidence that the competencies in Firm A and Firm B were well integrated into the values and norms of the trainees. That is, the specifically segmented and labelled behaviours *per se* are not active within the trainees 'regulation of the self', as evidenced by the fact that the trainees did not report assessing their *own* behaviour in these terms on a daily basis. However, trainees generally felt that as such the competencies overall did cover the main aspects of the work and behaviours needed for successful performance of the tasks they faced. They had few suggestions as to what could be added or changed in relation to the specific competencies. Nevertheless, the segmentation itself was viewed as alien to the experience of the work and thus the competencies have not been 'absorbed' into the mentality with which trainees face their daily work. It is also possible that because the appraisal systems are not evident, on a daily basis, most of the time their salience and potential to impact on ways of thinking about work experience was reduced. Nevertheless, the ratings recorded on performance appraisal forms were reported to be consequential in remuneration and promotion decisions, and trainees who wished to succeed in the firm must be seen to perform in a manner that did not result in poor scores. Consequently any criticisms, or poor ratings, that do occur on an appraisal form had to be attended to, and 'corrected'. Thus some sorts of behavioural outcomes are achieved by the appraisal systems. However, because of such issues as the delays in feedback, issues which seemed to reflect a relative lack of emphasis upon the process at this level of the firm, it appears that daily experience, such as comments from colleagues, is as integral, if not more so, to socialization, to shaping behaviour, as the formal appraisal systems.

1.2.1 The Importance of Social Skills and Norms in Performance Appraisal Systems As noted in the earlier section on recruitment, the ability to demonstrate certain social skills, and exhibit behaviour conforming to certain social norms, is essential to convince recruiters that one will be able to interact successfully with colleagues and clients. Both firms acknowledge this need further by including an assessment of such abilities in the competencies that are assessed in their formal performance appraisals (e.g. 'social skills', and elements of professionalism - as defined at Firm A).

Social norms, personality, and social skills all have an impact on the social aspect of working with other people. Of course, despite the aspirations of recruiters and personnel departments, sometimes, even within groups of people selected for their potential to fit in with other members of the organization, there will be clashes of personality. On the other hand, within the workplace social relationships form between people who get on significantly better with each other than they do with others. The formal evaluation systems aim to provide an objective measure of performance for all individuals but, in practice, informal evaluations - the general opinion one person has of another person - are evident in both firms, and do impact inevitably and perhaps rather obviously upon the formal rating systems. For example:

"I told him that he had problems working with women and then he was asking me to get the coffee all the time and I asked him if he was asking me because I was an Assistant or because I was a woman and he didn't like that and we didn't get on on the job and I got an absolutely atrocious rating form" (Audit Trainee, 1st Year).

"For example, this friend who left I had some jobs with him just before he left and he gave me absolutely glowing reports so although I've put them first, when he sees them the Manager's going to look at it and go 'You two are best mates (laughter) bloody obvious that he's going to put something like that'" (Audit Trainee, 1st Year).

Because of the stated competencies in the formal appraisal systems and the informal aspects that affect these formal systems, being like and liked by superiors are fundamentally important to how trainees are rated, via the formal appraisal systems in the firm and reinforces the grouping of alike persons within the firms.

1.2.2 Presentation to the Client in Performance Appraisal Systems The concept of the 'client' is central in the construction of the performance appraisal systems and as we discuss in detail in Chapter 5 is central to the constitution of concepts of professionalism. First, the timing of the bulk of the appraisal records for audit, that is the job review forms, is determined by a certain length of time performing on client work. Second, 'client service' is formally rated by both firms. Whilst the actual technical work performed is always checked by superiors and commented on, the appraisal systems ensure that behavioural aspects of conduct with regard to the client are also assessed. 'Social skills', and 'professionalism' are competencies that are deemed to be exhibited whilst performing client work, and, more importantly, to varying degrees (depending on the division the trainee is employed in - see Chapter 6) this work is executed in the presence of the client. Consequently the appraisal forms ask if the trainee works "harmoniously and effectively with clients and colleagues at all levels and has strong respect for individuals and their circumstances"; "Inspires confidence through appearance and personal presentation"; and " is able to deal with client staff at senior levels".

Technical ability, and the ability to pass the professional examinations are in a rather obvious way crucial to the success of trainees, but, equally, as formalised in the performance appraisal systems, trainees must perform more than just tolerably well in front of the client (and the more senior colleagues who will be completing rating forms) in order to be a successful trainee accountant.

1.3 Training

1.3.1 In-House Training Courses Training, by definition, is an attempt to alter individual behaviours. Trainees attend introductory courses as soon as they begin their training contract; exceptions to this are those who start their contract later than the majority of trainees. These trainees may have to wait until suitable scheduled courses occur. The courses initially cover basic technical skills such as book-keeping. Trainees in both firms also referred to sessions in their first few weeks which 'teach' them how to dress professionally, and in one firm, how to answer the telephone.

In Firm A there are two introductory courses. One is a five day non-residential course for those graduates who will be undertaking professional examination training (for GCC) straight after the introductory course. The other course is an eight day non-residential course for graduates who are taking GCC later in the training-contract year, and those (relevant) graduates who are exempt from GCC. After attending this initial eight day course trainees attend an international in-house, functionally specific (i.e. Audit or Tax or Insolvency) course. Those who go straight on to Graduate Conversion training at a tutor firm attend the international in-house course after sitting their Conversion examination.

In Firm B all trainees attend a 10 day book-keeping course at the beginning of their contract followed by an introductory residential course. Graduate Conversion study is taken via the Link method of study and the examinations will be taken the following summer. In both firms in-house training continues throughout the training contract.

1.3.2 Examination Tuition Courses Both firms send their trainees to external, private sector, tutor firms. Chapter 6, section 3, discusses how trainees are segregated into different modes of training. Consequently it suffices to state at this point that, regardless of mode of training (link, split-intensive, full-time), or GCC exemption status, trainees are part of a 'year' group. This grouping is a function of studying for, and sitting, examinations en masse with other trainees. As most trainees pass their examinations first time, and if not first then second time, the trainees remain with the same groups of people for their examination tuition courses, which enables an obvious 'year' structure to be maintained.

1.3.3 Ethics Training On joining the firms trainees receive binders of information which include their firm's professional code of ethics. Trainees reported that training on the professional code of ethics is covered, to some degree, as part of the examination syllabus at the tutor firms. However, other than maintaining client confidentiality and anonymity, trainees generally reported that ethical issues are not regarded as particularly relevant at their junior level although they do provide one of the few reference points for trainees to consider the role of the professional institute (the other, and more significant, being the examination process, see Chapter 5).

1.3.4 Presentation to the Client, and Social Skills and Norms Within Training Courses The previous sections have noted the importance of client service to the firm. Training courses also make explicit the attempt to ensure that the relevant behaviour displayed in front of clients is reinforced and developed. Trainees in both firms referred to sessions in their introductory courses which 'teach' them how to dress professionally, and in one firm, how to answer the telephone. The reactions of trainees to the formalised instruction in dress codes were broadly negative: trainees that commented on these courses tended to regard them as insulting and/or amusing (cf. Coffey, 1993). This confirms that trainees, as indicated in their interview behaviours, are already aware at this early stage of the need to present a well-dressed, polite, efficient persona in a business context. For example:

> "On the first day we did have a day like that of being told what to wear which I thought was rather stupid really" (Audit Trainee, 1st Year).

> "I know on my first course we had sort of how to answer the telephone...really it gets a bit patronising at times" (Audit Trainee, 1st Year).

The resentment of trainees towards this formalized instruction in dress codes seemed to reflect their views that either such points were obvious and therefore insulting or that indications of appropriate dress were readily gathered from those peers with whom they worked. Yet the possibility that a new trainee might be sent to a client very soon after starting work at the firm seems to operate as sufficient justification in both firms for such instruction to be provided to reinforce the norms of presentation to clients.

1.3.5 Informal Aspects of Training Courses: Socializing as Socialization
Formal tuition is not the only tool for socializing trainees at training courses. In both firms trainees find that their first intensive contact with other people from the firm is with trainees who are in the same (inexperienced) position as themselves. The residential courses were reported to be intense experiences where people are expected to 'work hard and play hard' often in precisely these terms; after each day's training, trainees often found there were social events arranged. Otherwise generally long evenings in the bar seemed to be the norm. This reinforced the expectation that a trainee should be a 'high energy' person (able to commit a good deal of effort and long hours), whatever the situation. In addition, the intensity of the contacts, and the opportunity to meet with like-minded people in the same situation as oneself leads to friendships being made that tend to remain beyond the training course. These friendships form a social base and work network for trainees:

"in a work environment...it's quite hard to get to know people whereas on a residential course you finish in the evening. They organise a few social activities, go out for a few pints or whatever, you get to know people after a while, and also Thisfirm's recruiting policy is they obviously get people of similar nature and similar outlook and similar backgrounds so that it's quite easy to relate to that in other people...There was about 15 that joined at the same time and quite regularly we still go out together as a group" (Audit Trainee, 2nd Year).

The norms and values of these groups, as they develop, are then likely to continue to impact on the trainee. Many trainees report that the experience of working with young, like-minded people is one of the 'best' things about their experience in the firm and the sense of friendship and bonding with one's peers is certainly strong:

"the amount of really close friends I've developed this year is quite surprising because I've got a hell of a lot of really good friends from work. The majority of time out I don't go out with my friends I've had previously, they are Thisfirm friends and that's something that I would never have thought of really... I've been quite surprised how quickly I've totally, I went away with a couple of Thisfirm lads this last weekend to Dublin which was very good. I've been quite surprised how many good friends I've made" (Audit Trainee, 1st Year).

"you are dealing with a group of people who are your own age with potentially similar background with possibly similar interests and that you're all going through it together and it's kind of like being at school to a great extent. Especially when you're at college because you're going in at every morning at nine o'clock and you go home at four and you have break and you go outside, so yes, that's probably the best thing, that you're doing it as a group" (Audit Trainee, 2nd Year).

Whilst socializing is certainly not the same as socialization, it is indeed part of the socialization process. Social skills are part of the recruitment profile of the firm: they employ people who enjoy being in the company of others, who are young and have recently enjoyed the social life of an undergraduate, and generally wish to continue enjoying their social life. The firms also arrange some social events. There are firm sports teams, and the firms plainly encourage socializing at residential courses (often providing generous allowances at the bar). In sum, the firms encourage a culture of sociability and socializing. The bonds developed between people at a social level meld people together such that feeling part of a 'team', to some degree, is increased in terms of daily work experience. The value of this effect is reflected more formally in the concept of 'away days' which are also reported to have the effect of 'bringing people together'. Both firms utilise this concept. Firm B has more away days as the divisional departments in audit have their own 'away days'.

Much of the socializing that takes place is spontaneous and involves trainees telephoning each other to find out who would like to go out on a certain evening (often Friday evening). Tax people tend to go for a drink after work or a meal at lunch-time. Occasions such as promotions, examination results and people leaving the firm also provide plenty of justifications for social events. After the first few months of arranged events socializing is more spontaneous and so those people who have identified with other people will be involved in these spontaneous arrangements. Those who have friends in the area outside of the firm, or a spouse or partner, may be less involved. These groups will strengthen or disband as people find out more about each other: their likes and dislikes etc., and as people leave. As noted above, the structure of the training contract and the in-house and examination training creates 'years' of trainees, and it is often peers from one's 'year' with whom trainees will socialize. However, in Firm B the divisional departmental structures also structured the patterns of socializing. On these occasions fitting in with the values, beliefs and behaviours of senior colleagues, as well as peers, is important.

Trainees rarely socialized with their opposite numbers in other firms and few reported involvement with the student societies or activities of the profession. However some exceptions were described, namely people who knew other firm's trainees from University; and several people at Firm B mentioned that they did mix with trainees from the other firms at the tutor firms but this was untypical. If the ICAEW student society ball is attended, it was suggested that, as a result of the firm's supplying separate rooms with drinks for their people, 'mingling' is not the norm. Consequently trainees are generally isolated from other trainees and less likely to have their views, behaviours etc. influenced by external sources. As we note in Chapter 5 identification with the firm mediates the involvement with the idea of 'profession' to a significant degree.

1.3.6 Mentoring The value of informal 'training', of feedback and advice on a daily basis, was acknowledged by both firms. The role of facilitator/tutor is recognised formally such that both firms appraise the 'people development' abilities of their professional staff. In addition, or perhaps as a deliberate replacement for the informality and possible inequity implied by the everyday notions of mentoring, Firm B, which in other areas also seemed to have invested in HRM techniques to a greater extent than Firm A, operated a formal mentoring scheme. Each new trainee was assigned a 'mentor', a recently qualified person, as a point of contact for information, and who was intended to assist the trainees in completing firm specific documents that set out the 'skills' the trainee must have achieved by the end of their first year. The scheme was not regarded by the trainees as especially successful at the time the research was undertaken. For example, the nature of audit work meant that opportunities for mentor and trainee to meet were often rare. Also, turnover of recently qualified staff meant that trainees were often in the position of their original mentor, and even successive mentors, leaving, sometimes without replacement. Some trainees reported that the mentor scheme was useful for them. Often, however, trainees suggested that it was easier to discover as one went along who to approach for certain information and general guidance.

2. Other Modes of Socialization

2.1 Informal Training

2.1.1 Advice and Feedback Most trainees have not experienced audit, tax, or insolvency work before joining their firm. Those with some idea of what the work might entail had a general notion that the work tends to be routine and monotonous in the first year(s). They are put onto client work early in their first year (sometimes within a few weeks, depending on training course arrangements), and are usually in-charge of an audit by their third year, if not sooner. Consequently trainees are reliant on information and feedback from their seniors, and any information they can remember from the training courses they have been on, in order to accomplish successfully the tasks they are set.

Trainees reported that the instruction and feedback they get on a daily basis was the most essential for their development. Unsurprisingly some seniors were regarded by their juniors as better at this than others. Those in senior positions that are able to 'empathise' effectively with the trainee are valued by the trainees:

> "When you learn how to actually do an audit you learn that actually out whilst you're doing the job and if you're working for somebody who's a good in-charge who can explain things then you learn absolutely loads" (Audit Trainee, 3rd Year).

Such feedback is certainly not restricted to technical issues. For example this trainee reported that some of the other trainees regarded him as 'cocky'. Whilst on one audit job he was reprimanded for his informal way of assisting a client in her preparations for the audit:

> "like I say I've been penalized for getting on well with people because they themselves don't get on well with people. So it's a bit unfair in that respect and it does de-motivate you a lot that. Because you think 'What's the point?'... It's made me quieter. It's made me hold back a lot more and it's made me if anything less friendly towards the client" (Audit Trainee, 1st Year).

As noted in the above section on Performance Appraisal; the degree to which personalities clash can affect the quality of working relationships, and thus can also affect the advice and feedback the trainees receive.

2.1.2 The 'Proactive Approach'   Although the role of the senior includes instructing trainees, the latter also learn that asking questions (of in-charges and colleagues not working on their job) is the appropriate way to act - waiting to be told can waste time, as it causes errors that might not be noticed until a later stage of the work. Again asking questions is only part of the requirement for success, who you ask is important too:

> "It depends entirely who you are working with. I personally always asked questions. That was, I suppose that was because the person I worked with first of all said 'Don't sit there and struggle, just ask' so I got into that habit which is quite a good habit in a way because at least, well it might annoy them sometimes if they're busy, but at least you know what you're doing and you can just see why you're doing it rather than, there's nothing worse than doing something and not knowing why you're doing it. So, yes, I think it is just this learning curve, different people, different jobs and eventually it all falls into place" (Audit Trainee, 3rd Year).

Thus trainees learn that they have to be proactive and responsible for their own development. The fact that trainees are also formally responsible for ensuring their job review forms are completed, and appraisal arrangements are taking place when they should, emphasises that the firms value personal responsibility.

3. Further Consequences of Formal and Informal Socialization Process

3.1 Locating the Trainee: Hierarchical Organizations

The 'year' structure and identification with this group also quickly initiates the trainee into the nature of being in an organization with a definite hierarchical structure:

> "I've never felt like a student. You've always known your position because you've always been, we are, it's not like a normal job, a lot of jobs where you come in, you're the one person, you join, at whatever time of the year, and eventually, we're always in years. It's very like being back at school, you're all in a year, you all belong to a year. So everybody knows where you do stand. So as you progress up then you do. I've never really felt like a student as such just sort of further down the pile really (laughter), it's just a case of moving up" (Tax Trainee, 3rd Year).

"You're not treated with very much respect in the office because even when you join you might be under the impression for a short period of time that you've made it but in actual fact you are right at the bottom of the pile" (Audit Trainee, 2nd Year).

In Firm B the departmental structure leads to junior members having more contact with managers than in Firm B. In both firms, however, trainees discern that managers and partners are more distant from their own experience as trainees than the qualified seniors. For example:

"it appears to me that once someone becomes a Manager in general it's like they seem to lose all empathy" (Audit Trainee, 2nd Year).

"Until recently here in this office I was told the partners never mixed with anyone below senior level because they thought it was necessary to instil authority, and they couldn't mix and if they did, by mixing socially with people on an evening on these social events we have that it would be seen to, you'd lose your respect for them" (Audit Trainee, 1st Year).

In both firms, there is little contact between junior trainees and partners. The patently pyramidal hierarchies of the firm illustrate that in order to be successful within the firm one has to move up the hierarchy or move out (Harper, 1988): one has to demonstrate all the social skills and technical skills that senior people recognise as essential, and one has to make sure one's skills are noticed by those with the ability to promote people. The structure highlights and symbolises the point that only a few of those who join the firm can hope to achieve the position of manager, and even less will be made partner. Whilst these statistics make explicit the certainty that it is essential to be open to opportunities outside the firm, it also highlights that most people do leave the firm and that one has to compete for places if one wishes to remain with the firm. This situation is reinforced by the fact that the trainees are told that they have only one opportunity to take and pass GCC. If they fail trainees know that they are expected to leave the firm. This experience communicates to trainees, from an early stage, that 'failure is not tolerated'. Trainees have to (learn to) accept or at least tolerate, their junior status. They also have to (learn how to) behave in terms of their status. More specifically they have to judge such issues as; how far to assert their own point of view, and whether it is appropriate for them to talk casually/jovially with the most senior members of the firm.

3.2 The Gendering of Trainees' Experience

The compilation of the hierarchy also makes visible the male-dominated experience of trainees in the firm. Trainees do comment on the lack of women at manager and, particularly, partner level. Although unsurprisingly more female interviewees commented on this, male trainees also recognised this as an issue, for example:

> "you hear all these stories about sex discrimination at work and it just doesn't exist here.. Saying that it probably gets harder at later levels, I think there is a handful of female Partners in the firm out of several thousand" (Audit Trainee, 3rd Year).

The likelihood of career progression for women in the firms is viewed as problematic by the female trainees for various reasons. The culture in both firms is seen as 'masculine' and the chauvinism that is experienced is obviously unsettling:

> "Things like we went out for a training lunch and all the men started talking about football so I was just playing with my salad and thinking 'Oh God, this is really exciting' (!) and then he just turned to me and said 'Oh are you bored, well you can talk about shopping with Jessica' but he wasn't really joking, that was the annoying thing (!). I was like 'Oh, OK' ... Little things like that. It wouldn't affect your work day to day but, I don't know, it's just like the underlying..." (Tax Trainee, 1st Year, female).

> "It's been quite an eye opener that it is so sexist. One of my friends, she was seeing someone on the job, because it does happen because you don't really meet that many people outside the Firm and when the Firm was encouraging you to go out with people in the first week from the Firm, and then that's the people who you meet in NorthernTown and you've come to NorthernTown from different places, it's hard to meet other people so in her case she was seeing this guy and some of the male Managers were giving him a bit of stick about it by being a bit vulgar about it and then she's a really nice girl and really proper and one of the Managers got his Secretary to ring her up and ask if they wanted double rooms in the Hotel and we found that quite appalling. I said to her that she should have complained to the Personnel Department about it, but again she didn't want to rock the boat and stuff" (Audit Trainee, 1st Year).

There was also a claim that 'Northern' clients (both our offices were located in the North of England) didn't always appreciate a female auditor:

"I don't know whether it's the same in other Firms. I also think it's quite, especially later on, it's a lot harder for, having spoken to women managers about this it's a lot harder for women to make it in accountancy because you're expected to build client contacts. It's just a lot harder especially not maybe if I was in the London office it wouldn't be but all our clients in [NorthernTown] are heavy manufacturing clients and they are all like male F.D.'s and F.C.'s and it's just hard for them to accept a woman especially in a managerial role. Probably not so at my level but having spoken to Managers who are women I don't know whether that's going to change in the near future, hopefully" (Audit Trainee, 2nd Year).

Whether this is an accurate reflection of Northern attitudes, or a legitimating device used to maintain the dominance of male accountants in senior positions in the firms is an open question (Grey, 1998).

The demands on the time of trainee accountants are such that work, rather than personal life, tends to be the dominant factor in their lives (see Section 3.5 below). Many trainees foresaw the lifestyle of a manager not fitting easily with the demands of a young family. Indeed the following trainee hypothesised that even a trainee with a family would have a difficult life:

"At the moment at my level I think it's pretty hard to come home and have other responsibilities say to your family or if you've got children because you are having to work overtime in the busy season. You are having to study hard during examination time so it's not like a nine to five or half five job at all" (Audit Trainee, 2nd Year).

As noted above 'the client' is central to the working experience of trainee accountants. Consequently, those trainees who commented on alternative working arrangements felt that part-time work or flexi-time was not appropriate or feasible as the client could be inconvenienced (cf. Dirsmith *et al*, 1997, pp.17-18). That alternative methods of working are not 'visible' as an option (even if, in fact, they might be offered by the firms) emphasises the nature of the firms as organizations that are structured in a way that makes heavy demands on what trainees come to call their 'private time'. We examine this issue further in the later sections of this chapter on 'time-management' (Section 3.5) and 'success' (Section 4). However, it suffices to say that whilst male and female trainees appear to be equally time pressured at work, and trainees generally do not have the non-work responsibilities that senior staff have (responsibilities that often demand more of women), in these other ways (perceived career possibilities; chauvinism) male and female trainees do experience the firm differently.

3.3 Co-operation and Competition

As Hanlon (1994) has observed, there is 'an atmosphere of competitive individualism' in Big Six firms. In our firms the desire to be 'rated' does exist and this leads to trainees striving to give an impression of 'doing their best' at all times:

> "Our year is ... extremely competitive amongst each other. Not in terms of like we want to, just for recognition really. I don't know, it's all the people in our year. I don't know if it's the same with all Graduate kind of you come out of University and you feel to some extent insecure in your own abilities and the real world" (Audit Trainee, 3rd Year).

This 'striving to be the best' is also encouraged by the emphasis the firms place on terms such as 'quality' and 'excellence'. Also, at professional examination training courses there is the certainly the aspiration to do at least as well as one's peers and to some degree to do just that bit better:

> "And it depends on the groups - the spread of results. I think our group wasn't too bad, we were quite friendly and the spread wasn't too bad. Some people did well and others weren't too bothered about it. I think other groups could be a bit more competitive" (Tax Trainee, 3rd Year).

Competition is viewed as self-evident, but so is co-operation. Trainees often socialize together, some share rented accommodation with colleagues, they may discuss examination questions together, and they certainly discuss other work-related issues (e.g. who is good to work for, who is a bad client). If the technical experience of one trainee is lacking but she knows a colleague who has the knowledge/experience she currently lacks, generally she will contact that trainee and ask for advice, and, moreover, the very processes of competitiveness also create bonds of collegiality or comradeship between trainees.

As we noted above the trainees readily perceive that the organization is hierarchical. Trainees are at the first stage of their careers and are looking to be successful. They also enjoy the company of colleagues, and, more fundamentally, need each other in order to get their jobs done. In sum, they are in a situation that demands both co-operation and competition, and in the knowledge that other people will be being co-operative and competitive to various degrees. In our interviews with the trainees only a few trainees referred to personal experiences that they could describe as 'back-stabbing' and 'office politics'; matters of office politics more commonly referred to issues such as who had got on a 'good' job or client, who was unfortunate enough to have to be doing stock-taking at the week-ends and who was good or bad to work under - many of these details were regarded by trainees as signs of favour or disfavour within the firm. This is not to say that more colourful examples of 'back-stabbing' do not take place, rather it is that at the level of trainees office politics are relatively unimportant although particular events could provide topics of conversation between trainees. What is clear is that the training process is a matter of both co-operation and competition, and that trainees exhibiting an excess of one behaviour, to the exclusion of the other, would be unlikely to succeed.

3.4 Presentation of the Self: The Client

Trainees are put onto client work within the first few months, if not weeks, of their training contracts. Consequently they also have to appear competent in front of the client and their seniors at this early stage. Trainees report that some clients (the 'good' clients) are pleasant to work for, they are tolerant and have records prepared in advance of their visit, others are the opposite:

> "So that's what can make or break a job really; what information the client provides and just really how you get on with the client" (Audit Trainee, 2nd Year).

However, until several months have passed and clients have been experienced and stories swapped, the client remains 'unknown'. For the sake of self-esteem, appraisals, and for the firm, the trainee must appear 'professional'. Notions of 'professionalism' are discussed in Chapter 5, but it is useful to note here that the early experience of client interaction demands that the trainee 'appears' to be the right sort of person well before they are formally accepted as the 'right sort of person', that is before they are assessed by the ICAEW and qualify as a chartered accountant. In order to 'appear' to be the right sort of person trainees must dress as the client will expect and in a manner that reflects well on the firm, they must behave in a manner that respects the fact that the client is paying for the service (and, for audit, is having their daily business interrupted). In this way the trainee learns how to present a professional 'front' (Goffman, 1959) that the trainee, and her colleagues can rely on whatever the situation.

3.5 Time Management and Presentation of the Self

A significant element of this presentation of an acceptable self within the firms is time management. Time management is seen to reflect both trainees' 'professionalism' and their commitment to the firm. Trainees often state that punctuality is one element of professionalism (see Chapter 5), which includes not turning up significantly later than the employees of the firm that is being audited. Time management is also critical to other parts of the trainees' experience. One visible example is the advice trainees are given during training for the professional examinations that strictly timing each question is crucial to successfully passing the examinations.

Time sheets also highlight the value of time within the firm and overtime is often relied on to complete jobs, although charging all the hours that one might work on a job was not always the objective. Seniors would often come to understand that recording hours was a politically sensitive game in which meeting the hours set for a job means only recording the hours worked up to the budget set for the job. Hours worked in excess of the job would not usually be recorded in full by in-charge seniors (nor managers). Of course this type of 'falsification' of the hours logged onto an audit task, ostensibly for billing purposes, was no secret in the firms. It was rather expected that the qualified seniors, near-qualified seniors and managers would behave in this way and was taken to be a demonstration of commitment to the firm and career intent. For it to operate in this way others have to know that a person was making this 'sacrifice'. The more junior trainees, however, were not required to invest in this 'time game' partly because of their recognized commitments to significant periods of examination study after work, and partly because trainees have to gain and record their work experience on ICAEW training forms as part of their training contract.

Significantly, working long hours was also seen by trainees as a necessary condition of success within the firm. For example:

> "People that are unsuccessful are people probably that are unwilling to fit in with the long hours or the work commitment" (Insolvency Trainee, 3rd Year).

The culture of 'sacrifice' in that being seen to exceed 'office-hours' is seen as the 'done' thing such that:

> "It seems to be a little bit like that's how you have to be, to be successful you have to be seen to be here all the hours God sends...the way I feel is that it comes to half five I can't get up and walk out the door, I feel like I have to stop, which is mad" (Tax Trainee, 2nd Year).

Although trainees express their commitment to performing well, and working hard for their firms, the pressure to work overtime, even if the task at hand does not require it, is seen as unnecessary. Whilst individuals may not explicitly exert or even express the source of this pressure on each other, the demanding and competitive cultures of the firms do produce such pressures.

3.5.1 Time Demands and Personal Time In Firm A overtime is recompensed financially whereas in Firm B overtime for trainees is taken as time in lieu. As trainees become more senior their responsibility for jobs increases. In one firm in particular when trainees find themselves in-charge the culture of 'sacrifice' of personal time combines with the awareness that coming in on, or under, budget is paramount to their work, and themselves, being classed as successful. Whilst the in-charge can decide which evenings they are going to work overtime, and how long they are going to work over on those evenings, junior trainees are dependent on the in-charge to be sympathetic to non-work and study needs.

Trainees in both firms reported working many long and busy days, even if they were not required to do overtime. These busy days reduce the amount of time that is available to be spent away from the firm, such that examination study suffers, or relations with friends and family. Trainees also often reported that they are no longer able to participate in hobbies and sports enjoyed in the years before joining the firm. Not only is this resented, but it also bemuses many trainees. Some trainees recalled the emphasis given to demonstrating extra-curricular activities in the recruitment process only to wonder why they have recruited people who do excel at other activities only to deny them the opportunity to continue with this aspect of their life. Many trainees saw the heavy demands on their time as linked to examination study, and cope with this pressure by focusing on the temporary nature of these demands. However, as mentioned above, they also see success in the firm as being dependent on working long hours, so although the examinations process has a visible time-horizon, assuming success, trainees concede that, if they stay in the firm, their time will have to become increasingly devoted to work. A rejection of this scenario meant that some trainees did not foresee themselves continuing, in the long-term, with a lifestyle that is so demanding on their time.

Both firms urged through formal and informal means that trainees ensure their work and personal lives are 'balanced', such that they have adequate time for non-work aspects of life. However the demands of the firm and examination study make achieving this balance very difficult. Nevertheless, there were trainees who declared an ability to manage this, for example:

" If you want to do something find a gap somehow to do it. There's always time to do things if you want to do it. You work to live, not live to work" (Audit Trainee, 3rd Year).

Whether such trainees remain with the firm on qualifying remains to be seen. Given the pressure to be seen as successful it is difficult for trainees to complain officially about their workload. Also as temporal commitment is regarded as vital for success trainees often report that they believe it is wise not to "rock the boat".

4. The Meanings of 'Success'

The formal systems of appraisal impart some guidance as to what a trainee has to do and has to be, in order to be successful within the firm. However, trainees are also faced with a variety of daily experiences in which they have to gauge the 'correct' behaviour at that time. For example, trainees need to decide whether they should be exhibiting proactive or inquiring behaviour and showing initiative, or reactive behaviour and displaying respect for the status of another. Likewise trainees needed to assess when and how much to be competitive or co-operative. Also, trainees are exposed quite early in their contract to client contact and responsibility and thus have to try to assemble a coherent picture of what their role is whilst performing it. They are also left to their own devices to interpret and reconcile the various experiences of their new life: student, worker, social person with other non-work responsibilities.

Success in the firm depends not only on technical expertise and passing the professional examinations, but social expertise and the ability to present a 'professional' persona. Although failure of the professional Foundation level examinations usually leads to automatic dismissal, problems at the stage of later examinations (Intermediate and Final) may be tolerated if the trainee is generally rated sufficiently well. That is, those trainees who may find themselves struggling to get a first-time pass will be tolerated, and supported, if they have exhibited sufficiently that they are the right sort of person for the firm, have supportive mentors and their work for clients and presentation to clients is well-regarded.

Many trainees related that the archetype for success in the firm, based on the characteristics of managers and partners is one of technical excellence or, more commonly, of 'technical' competence *and* 'social' excellence, with partners being positioned especially in the latter category in terms of social networking and 'bringing in clients'. However success is seen as also dependent on sacrifice of time. Indeed as Seron and Ferris (1995) state:

> "In addition to credentials or licenses, performing professional tasks requires a system of social capital to ensure release from private obligation so that time is available to perform professional tasks" (p.25).

The lack of time for fulfilling involvement in personal commitments is certainly experienced at trainee level and therefore the training contract experience not only initiates trainees into the:

> "awareness that the boundary around the professional workplace is fluid and permeable" (Seron and Ferris 1995, p.26).

but also suggests to them that in a Big Six environment it appears to be 'work' that is dominant and thus personal time comes a poor second. For some trainees this professional life may not be appealing, as work and examination related experiences dominate the possibility of personal development in non-work areas of life. In Chapter 3 the notion of 'reality shock' was discussed: reality shock is defined as a mismatch of expectations of a situation and the 'reality' of experiences perceived such that one's hopes and expectations of a situation are not met. Time commitment demanded for success within the firms exceeds the expectations and hopes of many trainees. Equally the experience of being the 'bottom of the pile' can be a new and unwelcome experience for some trainees too.

Conclusion

This chapter has highlighted how, from the perspective of trainees of two Big Six firms, the process of socialization occurs:

- Socialization of trainees commences at the recruitment stage.
- Whilst 'technical competence' is a necessary condition of being a chartered accountant, it is not a sufficient condition. All formal processes of socialization: recruitment; appraisal and training emphasise the joint importance of passing the examinations, described as technical skills, and social skills that are considered to refer to dealing with and impressing clients.

- The trainee's persona has to be 'groomed' in terms of dress codes, social skills as well as technical competence in ways that it is assumed assure clients and senior members of the firm that they are the right type of person to be an accountant (in general), and an accountant in Firm A or Firm B (specifically).
- Although the impact of formal appraisal systems within the firms is ambiguous and perhaps weak, they can serve to rationalise and reinforce the 'informal' judgements that peers and appraisers make about trainees. The formal and informal reinforce each other. Nevertheless, social norms of attitude, dress conduct and relations with peers are integral to the processes of appraisal, promotion and development of expertise.
- Trainees learn that client service is paramount, and that one's life has to be structured in a way that allows one to achieve this.
- Commitment to the firm is seen to be demonstrated by working long hours and a willingness to commit personal or leisure time to work.
- Trainees learn to know when to behave in certain ways: e.g. as a professional/responsible auditor respected by the client or as a trainee treated with little respect at the office; open and trusting or careful and guarded.

The above findings relate to the experience of *trainee* accountants. The work experience of these individuals will change to some degree on qualification. Some individuals will leave practice on qualifying. For those who stay with the firm the environment will begin to change as they take on more responsibility but it will also change as the people they have trained with begin to leave.

5 Organizational and Professional Socialization

Introduction

In Chapter 4 we identified and reviewed the processes of socialization that occur in the course of auditor training in two Big Six firms. It was noted that examination performance, whilst a necessary condition for advancement within such firm, was only one component of the socialization of trainees. In common with the findings of other researchers (Coffey, 1993; Harper, 1988) trainees were expected to conform to organizational norms defined in terms of, for example, time-keeping, dress codes, meeting client expectations and socializing with peers.

In this chapter we consider the relationships between the socialization processes of trainees, and the culture of the *organization* and of the *profession* in order to explore the thesis that:

> *The socialization of audit trainees is into organizational culture first and professional culture second.*

At the centre of this thesis is an examination of the changing identity of the trainee as he or she progresses in the firm. The thesis draws upon the idea that the professional knowledge that is conventionally assumed to define a professional person is supplemented by types of informal norms that exist within the specific firm context and which assist in defining appropriate professional behaviour.

For example, it is common to much of the Anglo-American (cf. Rueschemeyer, 1986) literature on the sociology of the professions, especially that which draws upon Weberian theorising, to highlight the central role of formal instruction and testing in defining the process of entry into a profession (Parkin, 1979; Johnson, 1972). In so doing, the professional body erects a barrier between the professional who is entitled to practice and the lay-person. Hence the concept of professional knowledge has been understood to serve as the defining characteristic of the professional person. Nevertheless, as we sought to show in the previous chapter, trainees experience their 'profession' through various processes of socialization in the individual firm, rather than by direct interaction and socialization with a professional institution. The culture of the firm provides the environment within which trainees must adapt themselves and acquire their 'professional' identity. Fitting into the firm in such a way as to attempt to secure progression within the firm implies as we have noted, integration with social norms that define appropriate modes of appearance, speech and other behaviours. As other writers on professions have argued (Becker, *et al*, 1961; Atkinson, 1983; Harper, 1988; Coffey, 1993) 'professionals' act in ways which define them as professional through their behaviours rather than simply their 'expertise'.

In this chapter we consider the relationship between these norms of behaviour which are defined largely at the level of the firm and the self-identification of the trainees as 'professionals'. We examine the discourse of 'profession' and 'professional' within our research sites: how and in what terms trainees conceive and define themselves as professional (if at all), to what extent these discourses reinforce or cut across specific organizational identities, and how these discursive practices are acquired and enacted. The specific organizational cultures of Firm A and Firm B are compared in order to gauge to what extent their individual 'corporate' cultures contribute in different ways to the formation and maintenance of a professional identity. By considering the discourse of profession within our two Big Six firms we reach an evaluation of Thesis 2 in terms of the possibility of separating professional and organizational socialization processes and evaluating their relative importance.

The chapter comprises three main sections. In the first section we consider how, and the terms within which, our interview subjects in Firm A and Firm B defined themselves as 'professional'. In the second section we focus upon the associations between trainees and their professional knowledge and training by considering the interrelationships that trainees delimit between their membership of a professional institute, their acquisition of professional knowledge and expertise, and their work, both in terms of present experiences and future employment plans. The final section considers the influence of specific organizational cultures by contrasting the corporate culture initiatives of Firm A and Firm B.

1. Presentation of (Professional) Self in Everyday Auditing

At the heart of our arguments in this section is the recognition that the overwhelming majority of our interview subjects view the idea of 'professional' as a reference to ways of acting rather than a state of being. In other words, in the conduct of interview discussions about profession and professional, trainees invariably adopted a mode of response that referred to *being professional* and then elaborated this in terms of appearance, modes of conduct (to, for example, clients), etc, rather than summarising their role as professionals or their views as to what it means *being a professional*. In the course of our programme of interviews the authors recognised that this type of responsive expression was being adopted. The interviewer attempted to ask trainees to discuss also their sense of being a member of a profession (being *a* professional) to ensure that interviewees had the opportunities to consider other forms of response; although care was also taken not to lead interviewees into discussions that were not on their own terms.

In his 1989 PhD thesis Harper, drawing upon Goffman (1959), described the behaviour of audit trainees in the terms of dramaturgical metaphor. He reported how certain behaviours correspond to 'front stage' activities in the sense of being performances in front of significant audiences. Certain behaviours were deemed unacceptable in front of the 'client'. For the trainees in our study, the significance of professional behaviour as a way of presenting activity rather than determining the content of that activity was clearly dominant:

> "Turning up next day for work, ready for work even though you're feeling like crap. It's not being unprofessional [for example] going out the night before and getting drunk" (Audit Trainee, 1st Year).

Of course, being sober is only a very small part of the professional activity; in this quotation the interviewee was relating his experience of only a few days prior to our interview with him. Nevertheless, the quotation captures through example a key aspect of the embedding of a notion of being professional. Professional is a way of conducting oneself that tends towards the giving of an impression: being prepared to work to the same standard as if one did not have a hangover becomes the key criterion.

The broader sense of being professional that emerged was connected to the idea of professionalism as appearance. Moreover, this notion of professional conduct was seemingly transmitted to the trainees in part through their formal appraisal procedures within the firm that we described in the previous chapter. For example, the following respondent, an audit senior in Firm A, described the firm's appraisal forms in the following terms:

> "there's other parts of the rating system where you talk about their professional conduct, their presentation and enthusiasm to learn, their desire to be inquisitive

as to what they should be doing to better themselves at what they do, how they work, and they are obviously very, very important in the first six months, year probably and to some extent might become less important like with the guy who dresses smartly it's quite crucial to catch i.e. does he give a professional impression to the client. It's probably quite crucial to catch early on to make sure that he's not continuously going through giving the impression to the client that he doesn't know what he's talking about" (Audit Trainee, 3rd Year).

It was clear that these forms reinforced the notion that 'professional' referred to a trainee's personal appearance and conduct, especially with the client. For the "guy who dresses smartly", the need to monitor and control professional conduct is apparently reduced, but for others the requirement to ensure they are not giving the wrong impression to clients is crucial.

As noted in the previous chapter, trainees in both firms received instruction in a series of personal conduct and appearance issues:

"qualities such as courtesy, punctuality, commitment, turning up looking tidy, presentable ... not sort of smelling of beer (laughs)" (Audit Trainee, 3rd Year).

To that list might be added adopting a 'professional' signature on audit papers, drafting letters and internal memoranda in a business-like way, acquiring a firm handshake, answering telephone calls in an 'efficient' way and adopting the recommendations of the firm's editorial and document style guides in external correspondences. On each of these matters, trainees received either formal instruction or documentation, although as we have noted the reception by trainees of instruction on matters such as make-up was not often well received (cf. Coffey, 1993).

The transmission of this notion of 'professional' was not, of course, conducted solely through formal instructions and the appraisal criteria defined by the formal ratings systems, although we would suggest they have played a significant role in constituting the ideas of professionalism we observed. As many respondents noted following the behaviours of immediate superiors provided the most direct route towards assuming the norms of professional conduct and pursuing a career with the firm:

"Giving the manager confidence in you, giving the client confidence in you. I think most people here are wanting climb the ladder and so the more they can give off that aura of professionalism then they do" (Insolvency Trainee, 4th Year).

"[Y]ou've got to almost try and impress people and every time you get given a job even if it's only a minor job you've got to try and put effort into it even if it's just photocopying or faxing, you've got to make sure you fax it to the right person and you get it back and keep them posted what's happened with it" (Audit Trainee, 1ˢᵗ Year).

This identification of the norms of professional conduct with the *firm* is perhaps unsurprising. But the degree to which this relationship is affirmed by our respondents does suggest that the assumption of an individual professional culture distinct from that of the firm is highly problematic; professional norms are translated through the firms' internal training courses and appraisal processes into the attributes and behaviours that are likely to result in progress within the firm. Perhaps nowhere is this relationship between being professional and firm interests articulated so well as in the centrality of the construct of the 'client' in audit firms: the point of reference for most discussions of professional conduct centres upon behaviour towards the 'client':

"For the firm in general the clients are everything and probably one of the quickest ways to go and get yourself out of the firm is to go and really upset a client, and that boils down to professional conduct" (Audit Trainee, 3ʳᵈ Year).

As the above quotation illustrates, the idea of unprofessional behaviour is most often considered in terms of inappropriate speech or "general rudeness to clients" and indeed it was noticeable many of the "atrocity stories" (see codes) related to us by interviewees most often related to inappropriate behaviours in front of clients during audits. For example, one interviewee in Firm A described:

"I heard a story of someone who threatened a client with saying 'if you don't find this bit of information I'll qualify your accounts' and this was some junior person - all the client will do is 'phone up the Manager or the Partner and say 'what is going on?'" (Audit Trainee, 3ʳᵈ Year).

Another audit trainee reported:

"somebody blew up at a client once, not a Manager, somebody at the level that I am now, not in my years, going back years ago and I think that wasn't viewed as being particularly professional because it a) annoyed the client intensely, and it just created an awkward situation..." (Audit Trainee, 3ʳᵈ Year).

In neither quotation is the detail of the 'story' very vivid and, in both quotations there is the implication that the events occurred before the respondents joined the firm and they had heard the story through others. Both stories may very well be apocryphal, exaggerated or, if true, founded upon the *same* story, but the 'moral' of both in terms of behaviour towards clients is apparent: the perception that their firms address most issues of 'professional' in respect to attitude and conduct to the status attached to the discourse of the clients.

The impression given to clients is then a key organizing principle for the practice of professionalism. For the firms this manner of defining professionalism serves to protect the client-customer base. But it also serves a purpose for the trainees when they are presenting a front to clients and performing their audit tasks. This point is readily appreciated when it is recognised that audit trainees often have to address and 'interrogate' the senior accountants and managers of clients very soon after starting their training contracts. An audit trainee will typically start his or her employment after university (or, perhaps, after a 'year out') and commence auditing in the context of very little knowledge of auditing or indeed, if the graduate has a non-relevant degree, of double entry book-keeping. In short, trainee auditors might frequently face situations in their first year where they are asked to execute tasks and ask questions of the client's company accountants and other senior managers about which they have only a very limited understanding. Yet such trainees are expected to appear credible, knowledgeable and competent:

> "It's a very young organization and I know myself when I went out with this [trainee] there was just two of us and it must have looked quite strange, two young lads wandering in to audit their [the client's] financial statements" (Audit Trainee, 2nd Year).

> "It depends on who your clients are but we've got a lot of clients back in Newcastle and if you go up there and start being cocky or like a typical kid straight out of university then you can cause some friction that people don't want" (Tax Trainee, 2nd Year).

By adopting 'professional' modes of conduct, audit trainees deal in part with their perceived problems of youth and credibility. The 'image' given to the client is viewed as the main rationale for the assumption of professional conduct:

> "[t]he way that you speak and the way that you act at a client just to promote the image of knowing what you're doing and being competent at your job" (Audit Trainee, 3rd Year).

Although in this section we have attempted to analyse the meanings that trainees construct for profession, it is important to note that a discourse of professionalism was more likely to emerge in a context of criticising behaviours than as a significant form of praise. Despite the emphasis given to professional conduct, the vocabulary of 'profession' and 'professionalism' was not necessarily viewed as an important element of the everyday discourse of the auditor, and was certainly much less prevalent than the discourse of 'the client', albeit that there were particular linkages between these discourses. Given our limited research into the settings of the Big Six firms it is difficult for us to be definite, but many of our respondents commented that the term professional arose mainly in quite specific contexts. Most of these contexts we have already considered: formal appraisal, in-house training courses, general advice and learned behaviours on conduct towards 'clients'. Moreover, in so far as the discourse of acting in a professional way had an active part in the everyday discourse of the auditors and others within the firm it often assumed importance in the context of critical commentary upon certain aspects of an individual's work or behaviour rather than being offered as a note of positive approval. This particular attribute is well illustrated in the following comment from a third year audit trainee in Firm A:

> "I don't think it's bandied around a lot but (pause) I think, well having said that I've just told someone off (laughter) and said 'It doesn't look very professional' but...".

As Goffman's analysis suggests, then, a key accomplishment of the trainee is the 'art of impression management'. The professional is a character (Goffman, 1959, p.203) that trainees are expected to stage for their clients and also their immediate peers. It is a role that most trainees know they are 'playing' rather than 'being', especially in those contexts where certain actions are played out amongst themselves and out-of-sight of the client:

> "I bought some after-shave balm this week and got a free Frisbee with it and when I got back to the office, I was sticking this Frisbee in my bag and a Manager walked past, took it out and started throwing it round the office. Now, to me I think that's great and probably most people wouldn't consider that very professional but at the same time I've worked for this guy on a job ... and he was the epitome of professional, you know, he was brilliant and I think it's a matter of being able to turn it on and turn it off" (Insolvency Trainee, 2nd Year).

Here the interviewee projects the image of unprofessional behaviours conducted in the office but away from the client. For a manager to conduct himself in such a way obviously has fewer risks - the likelihood of him being reprimanded for throwing a Frisbee around the firm's office was probably never very great. Nevertheless, the key point is the recognition by the trainee that professionalism is an attitude and behaviour that can be assumed or not as befitting the circumstances.

In this section we have argued that the identity of trainees as professionals is constituted in important ways by the principle of proper conduct. The attitudes and behaviours that we have outlined are transmitted to trainees through the firms' internal ratings or appraisal processes and the in-house courses which trainees receive on joining the firm. Of course, many of these informal modes of conduct are also reinforced by those in charge of audits whom trainees observe whilst at the 'client'. The relationship between the modes of conduct into which trainees become socialised and the concepts that make up the concept of being professional within the firm are organized to a significant degree through the construct of the client, in whose name many practices described as professional are performed. Nevertheless, this sense of being professional as a 'performance' or role for seniors within the firm and the client is widely understood by the trainees.

In the next section we move on from the discussion of being professional to consider the conception of being *a* professional engaged in acquiring professional knowledge and expertise, and how trainees perceive themselves as members or putative members of an old established profession.

2. Professional Qualification and Professional Expertise

In the above discussions of being professional we have presented an image of trainee socialization offering little in terms of a sense of a distinctive 'professional' identity in the sense that it can be distinguished from the firm's organizational socialization: being professional seems to be suggestive of norms of conduct in relation to dress, attitude and behaviour. Moreover these attributes seem to be understood largely as performances rather than constitutive of a significant sense of self or 'professional' identity. Perhaps such a distinction is itself problematical but in this section we consider how trainees express their relationship to their professional training and the institute that administers their training: in this case the ICAEW. We consider trainees' experiences of the examination process and the ways trainees relate their 'professional' training to their work within the firm.

2.1 Entering the Professional Firm

Although we have argued that the relationship to the firm is dominant in forming the conceptions of professional behaviour that trainees assume, in considering the apparent motivations and aspirations of those entering the firm a very different patterning emerges. For the majority of the trainees we interviewed the act of *qualifying* as a Chartered Accountant seemed to provide the overriding rationale for taking employment with a Big Six firm. The following quotation (from a first year audit trainee) expresses what emerged as a governing viewpoint:

> "I think it is, without being too corny, a very good business qualification to have. It's got more standing. It's got more standing I think in my opinion than a lot of the research, well not research but M.A.s and things like that, that exist" (Audit Trainee, 1st Year).

Notwithstanding the everyday audit work that the trainees are expected to perform, the accountancy training is seen to provide another form of education for graduates, which seemingly offers a general business training. Allied to this viewpoint were a number of subsidiary issues.

First, many trainees conceived of their career (after qualifying) as a path that stretched beyond the firm; rather than actively choosing to be accountants or auditors, for some the decision to take employment with a Big Six firm and undertake the professional examinations was rationalized as a way of deferring difficult choices concerning their future career:

> "As I say it was initially just an experiment to see what would happen" (Audit Trainee, 3rd Year).

For others the choice to train as a Chartered Accountant was viewed as a means to pursuing definite careers after qualification in areas of general business, taxation or banking:

> "I was told by a number of people one of them whose father's a Partner in a Merchant Bank said if you wanted to go into Merchant Banking the best way in if you want to be a Partner ... is to be a qualified Accountant" (Audit Trainee, 1st Year).

Whether such advantages actually accrue to the qualified accountant is, of course, unclear. Other reasons for joining the firm were also given: the possibility of foreign travel and secondment abroad, for example. The perception that accountancy qualification 'opened' rather than limited 'choices' or career plans, however, was cited frequently. Indeed, some interviewees reported that their entry into the firm they considered to be almost a matter of drifting into a respectable form of employment with little specific consideration towards the work of accountants or auditors *per se*:

> "I think, I don't know whether it was just an Oxford thing but most people there tended either to go into Law or into Accountancy or into the City to do sort of Merchant Banking type things and the vast majority of people that I know have done one of those three things. There's a few people who didn't, so I probably just followed like a sheep the people from before me and did the same" (Audit Trainee, 3rd Year).

Secondly, for some trainees the apparent difficulty of entering employment in business directly was seen as the primary reason for opting to take the accountancy qualification route. In this regard, the relative lack of consideration given by Big Six firms to graduates with relevant accounting or management degrees as opposed to other degrees served as the foundation for entering business occupations through accountancy qualification:

> "At the end of the day I didn't really have an idea of what I wanted to do in the long term but I knew in the short term a Chemistry Degree probably wouldn't be that relevant to business, therefore go for Accountancy. It's the classic thing, get the qualification and then look for something to do" (Audit Trainee, 3rd Year).

> "Getting into industry seemed really hard ... I feel that they would probably go for people with Management Degrees or Accountancy Degrees" (Audit Trainee, 3rd Year).

Whether such a seemingly slender sense of attachment to the firm remains with trainees once they have qualified is unclear, and beyond the scope of the present study, although we did note that those close to qualifying often expressed the desire to wait for any developments (or 'signs') within their firm before moving to external employment. The enticement to discover whether a long term career within their Big Six firm was a possibility seemed to be difficult to resist after three intensive years of training. On qualifying there was a general understanding that those who were regarded as destined for advancement within the firm would be given the 'sign' by the partners.

Nevertheless, our research suggests that the relationships trainees perceive between themselves and both the firm and the 'profession' would be best described as instrumental. This is in no sense a moral judgement on any parties involved, merely an observation that the notion of qualifying as an accountant and then moving into careers perhaps unattached to accounting seems to provide an overriding rationale for training. Whether such a finding is structured by interviewees' own perceptions of the 'image' of accounting is unclear, but it is worth noting that, while many interviewees would comment favourably upon their experiences as employees of Firm A or B, no-one expressed any sentiment that would suggest that they *enjoyed* auditing (those employed in tax departments might comment favourably on their work task) while many comments to the contrary were noted.

We would, therefore, suggest that although the ideals of professionalism we outlined in the previous section are allied to formal and informal norms of conduct defined and shaped by the firm, the commitments that trainees' express to the 'profession' through an identification with the firm is undercut to a significant extent by this instrumental relationship that trainees assume toward the accountancy qualification. Wider cultural beliefs concerning the value of accountancy as a general business qualification shape the attitudes that trainees bring towards their employment and indeed, their initial decision to apply to Big Six firms. Whilst this situation might be considered as an outcome of successful market action by accountancy firms (see Chapter 2) it also serves to undermine any perceived allegiances towards the firms' themselves and the accountancy bodies. The dominant message from the trainees is that the firm is a vehicle to the achievement of the professional qualification, and qualification is in turn a vehicle for career options and success.

In the next section we consider the narratives our interviewees gave us of the professional training and examination process, and the relationships that trainees establish between their professional training and their experiences of working within their firms.

2.2 Examination Training and Professional Expertise

Although it is common for the first few weeks of a training contract to be taken up with in-house 'induction' courses, the place of the professional examination process in the experience of the trainees is soon emphasised through the introduction or reinforcement of such techniques as double-entry bookkeeping. Professional examination training introduces one of the first bases of group or sub-group identification within the firm: between the relevant and the non-relevant graduates. As noted earlier, the trainees with relevant degrees are put upon a different examination track, taking the courses provided by the external professional examination tutors (in this case Financial Training and Accountancy Tuition Centre) at different times and at a more advanced stage (Intermediate) of the professional training process. Detailed discussion of all of these issues is deferred to the next chapter.

Although we have emphasised in previous sections that many of the conceptions of *being* professional that interviewees articulated were allied to issues of conduct and appearance to clients, the centrality of passing the professional examinations is well understood by trainees both in terms of the possibilities for advancement within the firm and the opportunities externally for exploiting the accountancy qualification. Moreover, trainees were made aware of the significant cost that their employing firms pay to the external tutoring agencies and of the cost to themselves if they have to re-take examinations at their own expense. Both our firms operated, in theory, a stringent policy towards succeeding at the Graduate Conversion Course (GCC) stage: many trainees commented upon the possibility of being 'fired' if they failed GCC. This certainly did happen during the period of our research, but in both firms we found there were exceptions made for those who 'just failed', although not in a consistent manner. At the Intermediate stage the possibility of being asked to leave the firm for failure in the professional examinations was also genuine, although at the Finals stage there was a much more tolerant approach towards not passing first time; a disposition reinforced by an ambiguous attitude on the part of qualified audit firm staff (and communicated to trainees) towards the emphasis in the Final examinations towards 'Business Skills' and 'Case Studies'.

Trainees, therefore, have few doubts as to the importance of passing the professional examinations. For some trainees, albeit a small minority, being a professional accountant was identified with having succeeded in passing the ICAEW examinations:

> "I don't think you've got a right to sort of feel as though you're superior until you've, even until you've got the, not superior but feel as though you've actually achieved something until you've got the qualification, only then really I think you're, you're a professional" (Audit Trainee, 1st Year).

Although the above quotation does not express a dominant view in terms of the articulation of professional and professionalism, accounts of the experience of the 'pressure' of the professional examination process upon the trainee were endemic. Given the expectations that trainees work overtime and, in many general ways, express their commitment to the firm's norms in term of blurring the boundaries between work time and personal time (see previous chapter), the expectation that the trainee study in his or her own time during evenings and at weekends, as well as perhaps take examinations on a

Saturday morning on the tutoring firm's premises, made the presence of the professional examination process seem constant, insistent and pervasive:

> "[W]hen you're doing the professional exams you just have no other life at all ... and then when you come back you wonder what you did before you started because you've got so much time on your hands" (Tax trainee, 2nd Year).

> "I don't think people properly take it into account how much you need to study outside work and when you're doing your overtime you can't necessarily just go home and open your books because you're too drained. I think people forget about that" (Audit Trainee, 2nd Year).

Of course, comments upon the examination process are always structured by the successes and failures of the individuals concerned. The second quotation above comes from a person who had just failed to pass the Intermediate stage exams. At the same time, however, many trainees considered that the problems of study and the commitments involved in terms of time and endeavour were underplayed by those within the firm who had passed and that, therefore, as the above quotation suggests, there was little support for trainees in terms of accommodating the requirements to do overtime with that of studying. Not all a trainee's time, of course, will be spent at a client's; at slack times of the year they may spend several days at the office, in theory a time to study. Some trainees suggested, however, that such time was rarely spent studying but absorbed in tasks such as photocopying and 'calling over' accounts.

In this context the examination process is seen by trainees to take on the character of a 'trial of strength'. Auditors, trainee and qualified, freely admit that the demands of work and study make very significant demands upon 'working time' but the process once accomplished by some, by definition those who are able to remain with the firm and progress, is viewed as 'do-able' (if demanding) and changes to the work patterns of trainees are seemingly resisted.

In summary, the examination process assumes a central and important place in the trainee's experience of training. Passing the examinations might be defined by some as the process of being a professional, an experience structured by the terms of employment within the firm and the temporal commitments that work and study put upon the trainee. The stress that is laid upon passing examinations says nothing about the value that is put upon the content of the examination training received. Therefore, in the final part of this section we consider the linkages that trainees understand between their everyday work experiences and the 'technical' knowledge they are taught and examined upon through the professional examination process.

2.3 Professional Expertise and Everyday Work

In this section we consider a different aspect of the discourse of professions: the expertise that is transmitted to trainees through the examination process and the relationships perceived by trainees between the knowledge gained through the exams to the everyday work of the trainee in a Big Six firm. As the examination process is one of the key elements that is said to separate the 'professional' from the layperson, it would seem pertinent to consider how trainees value the knowledge and expertise they are taught by the professional tutoring agencies and tested upon by the professional bodies.

Many of our interviewees were eager to discuss the professional examination procedures that they were experiencing on the way to becoming qualified accountants, although it is more difficult to summarise the views and attitudes expressed into one coherent standpoint. For example, although all our respondents agreed with the sentiments expressed in the previous section, that the study for examinations was arduous and time-consuming on top of the 'nine-to-five' of auditing or tax work, there was some divergence of views concerning the merits of the knowledge imparted and its relevance to the work of the auditor or tax expert (see the following chapter for full details on the audit-tax distinction). Most agreed that in the initial phase the study involved in passing Graduate Conversion was often detailed and intensive in terms of particular topics of study, but also corresponded most closely to the study of 'academic' subjects they had experienced at university in their undergraduate degree. The rather obvious difference was the amount of attention given to bookkeeping techniques, a subject with which most would be unfamiliar. Even those with a relevant degree acknowledged that the amount of detail in the foundation accounting stage was much greater than on an equivalent accounting degree.

Views as to the relative importance of the knowledge attached to the study involved at the Intermediate stage attracted a wide range of views. Many saw the 'technical' knowledge as of some importance even if that importance was not always immediately apparent:

> "I think it depends what subject really. Say looking back to intermediate. There was things like the financial reporting paper was useful because you are using that sort of thing on a day to day basis so I think the technical coverage you get on the exams. is useful. With some of the other papers, tax as well I think

although saying that, I don't work in Tax I'm not using it regularly, you do need the knowledge of tax just to help you keep that in your mind when you're Auditing or whatever" (Audit Trainee, 3rd Year).

Some interview subjects who freely admitted to failing to see the relevance of the professional examinations were content to take the view that its relevance would unfold in due course. The degree of relevance perceived could be viewed as a compromise between the wide range of backgrounds and organizational contexts that those training to qualify as accountants inhabit. As one trainee commented:

"As an Auditor I guess the financial reporting is pretty useful and I can see how it directly relates all the stats and everything the auditing again and the tax you would need to know if you were in tax you need to have a general awareness of tax if you're in audit. The management subjects less so ... I don't think they are completely unrelated to your job at all. I don't see how they can really make them any more specific without kind of making them less relevant for people you know you're cutting out sections" (Audit Trainee, 2nd Year).

Across many of the interviews the notion of the examinations as 'technical' or addressing 'technique' was a dominant mode of description; the material tested through the examinations might be viewed as technical but not always 'practical'. Whether or not such a dichotomy is entirely valid the idea that the content of the examination process was not always "relevant" was a common form of criticism.

Yet the criticism that is implied by describing the professional exams as 'technical' was often accompanied by the view that the examinations were there simply to be 'got through'. For example, interviewees from both firms, especially Firm A, let us know that good performance in examinations in terms of winning prizes was not particularly valued by the firm; the examinations were there to be passed:

"I think the professional exams in terms of Firm A are seen more as a hassle that we have to go through rather than an actual benefit" (Audit Trainee, 2nd Year).

This perception that the technical content of the professional examinations and the belief that doing well in the examinations was not relevant to the firm was seemingly reinforced by the reactions of trainees to the schooling of the external tutoring agencies who were there to 'get people through' the examinations:

"They're [External Tutors] very helpful, they give you the massive study packs, plenty of questions to work through and they will tell the areas you need to know intimately. They were very directing you to pass the exams. The aim is for them to get you through the exams" (Trainee Auditor, 1ˢᵗ Year).

The term 'technical' seems to assume a dual meaning: technical knowledge relevant to the legal and regulatory environment of accounting, but also the idea of examination technique, ways of addressing examination questions so as to maximise the process of gathering pass marks. The sense that tutoring was oriented towards (the technique of) passing the examinations rather than understanding the technical material led on to the views expressed by a significant minority of trainees that the examinations process itself was simply a means of erecting a barrier to entry into the occupation (in the fashion of Weberian theory of professions). The examinations, to some trainees, seemed to lack consistent focus, especially in the Final stage. One recently qualified auditor commented:

"They gel only in the fact that you have to know all your intermediate stuff before you could contemplate doing Final. But having said that you could have done the Final a week after intermediate, given the set of exams that we've done. That seems to be the consensus that you needn't have learnt any of the new stuff because it just wasn't tested" (Audit Trainee, 3ʳᵈ Year).

There is a level of irony in that the 'new' material introduced in the Final stage was, we understand, intended to provide the kind of 'business skills' that graduates might require in employment outside of the accounting or auditing firm. Nevertheless, both hostility and confusion was expressed towards the aims and content of the Final stage examinations:

"I don't really think, I'm not totally sure that they know what they're testing by their exams. Maybe people always joke that way that when they join the Institute they're going to make it even harder for anyone else to pass" (Audit Trainee, 3ʳᵈ Year).

"I think it's partly, obviously you need the technical knowledge and they've got to test that you're up to date on that but as much as anything they're just used as a barrier to entry to the profession. It's just a way of making it harder to qualify" (Audit Trainee, 3ʳᵈ Year).

A number of our interviewees also expressed substantial degrees of cynicism about the way examinations are marked and how the pass rate is decided upon; it was clear that this subject was a prevalent topic of conversation amongst the trainees when studying at the professional tutoring agencies:

> "the way I perceive it works is there's only 60% of people who pass or something like that so in theory you could still get 90% but because of the way they limit entry, in practice you would never get 90% in an Accounting exam. I don't think unless they fudge the figures, but I think they do massage the pass mark and things like that to get a certain number of people through" (Audit Trainee, 3rd Year).

Of course, this is not to say that either the content of professional examinations is irrelevant to the work of auditors and accountants or that the examinations are simply an obstacle to limit the supply of accountants. Nor are we confirming that the pass mark system is 'fixed' in the way the above quotation might suggest. We would argue, however, that the experiences of 'professional' examination training in the two firms we studied and at the professional tutoring agency seem to shape these opinions among a significant proportion of the trainees. The emphasis upon 'getting through' structures an instrumental attitude towards the examination training that is notionally intended to provide the knowledge base for accounting practice. One consequence of this is the relationship between the trainee 'professionals' and the accountancy bodies, in this case the ICAEW, is mediated almost entirely in terms of the examination process: setting and marking of examinations, paying fees, etc.:

> "there's going to be rules and regulations which are Institute driven, certain stuff that they do that you need to pick up on. But by and large the only time you're going to hear from the Institute is to send in an application form, send them some money and they'll send you the results back" (Audit Trainee, 3rd Year).

Other areas where trainees perceive some relationship between themselves, their work and the accountancy body seem to be confined to two specific issues: compiling training records and receiving the Institute Handbook:

> "There is the Institute handbook which is distributed every year to staff. I would say you are basically just told to read it as well. I started to read it but I know a lot of people don't finish reading it" (Audit Trainee, 1st Year).

> "We have training records to fill in and that's for the Institute, that's part of gaining, becoming a member of the Institute when you qualify" (Audit Trainee, 2nd Year).

The first of the above quotations arose in the context of a discussion of professional ethics; in almost all cases the issue of training in matters of ethics was referred to in the context of the 'binder' each trainee received from the ICAEW and which they were supposed to read.

In summary, in the second section of this chapter we have examined the accounts trainees give of their interest and experience in the process of gaining qualification as a chartered accountant. We noted that many of our interviewees' initial commitments to professional training were oriented towards gaining a credential relevant to business training rather than the fact of being an accountant. This would suggest that the relationship between identification with both profession and firm is undercut by trainees' broader conceptions of their future career. The experience of professional training was described by many interviewees as an obstacle that firms expect trainees to overcome but which is not necessarily valued as a learning experience. The style of tutoring by the external agencies is widely interpreted as reinforcing the pressure to 'get through' the examinations. No doubt as a direct consequence of these experiences many trainees (but not all) see few linkages between the material they learn and are examined upon, and their everyday work within the firm and at clients. This may account for the widespread cynicism toward the examination process and its value: criticisms of the examinations - especially the Finals but also the process of changes introduced into the pass mark systems - were widespread. Outside of the examination process, trainees see few linkages between their work as 'professionals' and the accountancy body to which they aspire to qualify.

In the final part of this chapter we analyse some of the differences between our two research sites and how they may structure the experiences of trainees in ways that might suggest the 'making up' of the accountant may vary between Big Six firms.

3. Professional Socialization and Organizational Culture

In this section we seek to identify the cultural differences that existed between the two firms that we studied and how these may influence the process of professional socialization. We conclude with some assessment of the relative importance of the differences that we identified in comparison with the similarities that also exist between the two firms. As assurances of confidentiality were given to both the Big Six firms that participated we have chosen to alter some of the details given to us in interviewees' responses in order to maintain that confidentiality. There are, however, obviously only six

'Big Six' firms and it is conceivable that a keen observer of the accountancy scene might still be able to identify the firms concerned.

In considering a firm's culture there are many, perhaps too many, dimensions that might be considered: organizational structures, patterns of hierarchy and control, organizational discourses, organizational beliefs and values. We start by examining the beliefs and discourses that trainees express about their own firm, beginning with Firm A.

3.1 Firm A 'By Design': The Culture of Culture

In terms of trainees' assessments of their own firms, a very sharp distinction emerged between our two firms. Firm A was identified by a very particular and distinctive organizational culture that was pre-defined to a significant degree by trainees even prior to starting their employment with the firm. Firm A seems to demonstrate a strong commitment to cultural self-definition that reflects the influence of a corporate culture by design. We call this a 'culture of culture' to highlight that the idea of the firm 'having' a culture formed a significant part of the internal and external perception of Firm A, and it was indicated as having many of the following characteristics. Firm A was considered by many trainees to have an 'aggressive' and 'competitive' character; trainees saw Firm A and the Firm A type as identifying with a firm ethos that involved commitment towards an organizational "mission" to be the best of the Big Six firms:

> "Thisfirm have got this image I think of, they don't settle for second best, they want to be the best so and they'll do that bit more" (Audit Trainee, 2nd Year).

This representation of the Firm A auditor was sold in recruitment brochures and interview procedures to the extent of identifying Firm A almost as a brand. It was clear that many trainees saw the Firm A 'type' in terms that suggested it was almost for external consumption:

> "Firm A has a bit of a reputation for producing aggressive arrogant people and it is incredible the amount of people who actually believe it" (Audit Trainee, 3rd Year).

In one important respect the argument of the above trainee is borne out in that during the course of the interviews at Firm B it was not unusual to hear comments of this type about Firm A; the making of the firm myth seems to have significant effects outside of the firm's arena. Some interviewees in

Firm B claimed that they had not applied to Firm A precisely because of the "reputation" it had for competitive and pressured working conditions. To what extent these differences emerged in our study we will consider later but it is also important to note that in Firm A there was a distinctive polarity of positions taken on the Firm A image.

First, it was apparent that many trainees took on board the image of aggressive competitiveness when applying to Firm A and the presentation given to many potential applicants served to reinforce a distinctive image of the firm:

"They have a very good presentation package for the milk-rounds and the like ... It's high-tech it's really good and they put all this emphasis on the training they give and they are also very efficient throughout the process in communicating with you" (Audit Trainee, 3rd Year).

"Anyone can knock up a slide put it on acetate and stick it in a projector upside down. But when [Firm A] turned up they had, it was a projector, but it projected like a video image, it has ability to change, it's like computer graphics, it like moves" (Audit Trainee, 2nd Year).

The outwardly trivial detail of having a well-prepared presentation served to strengthen the notion of Firm A as 'dynamic and competitive' to those who had already gleaned that this was the distinctive style of Firm A. The cultural claim to competitiveness and self-belief seemed to extend to other aspects of the recruitment process. For example, it was apparent from several of our interviewees that Firm A staff sought to ascertain whether applicants would accept an offer to join the firm before an offer was made ("If I make you an offer will you accept now?"). This 'device', transparent to many of our Firm A interviewees, served to reproduce the discourse of offering employment to those who were viewed as Firm A types and who would, therefore, accept. Similarly, the idea of a distinctive Firm A type was also signalled to recruits by the claim that Firm A was less concerned with degree classification and A-level scores than the other Big Six firms: the 'type' was someone with the right 'hinterland'.

A significant majority of trainees presented the 'front' of a Firm A type in their interviews. The claim that Firm A people viewed themselves as 'the cream of the cream' might be an extreme illustration but the idea of Firm A staff 'trying harder', being 'prepared to work longer hours' even being 'more professional' was not uncommon. Significantly, some Firm B trainees described Firm A in these terms. For those trainees who took on board the Firm A's self-defined cultural identity the negative connotations of aggression and arrogance took on more positive aspects or could be re-defined into more acceptable virtues. Competitiveness could be interpreted as a 'demanding environment' or seen as part of the firm's 'high expectations' of their recruits:

> "I think some of the students at Universities are quite taken aback when you say 'I'm not in a position to comment on another Firm, if that's what you've heard well maybe it's true but in my experience it's this' and it's not so much aggression as self-belief and self-confidence" (Audit Trainee, 2nd Year).

This is not to say that recruits into Firm A were those who 'bought into' the Firm A image, as it were, 'wholesale': the types of reasons that interviewees gave for choosing their firm were common across Firm A and Firm B - often a sense of personal rapport and liking towards the interviewer seems to have been very important. One of the consequences of Firm A's designed culture was equally a reaction against the image of Firm A aggressiveness by trainees who were disenchanted with their employment in Firm A. For some this could be expressed as a denial that the external perceptions of the culture were at all accurate; Firm A was the same as the other Big Six firms, the hype might be different. As one trainee put it 'it's hard to have that sort of perception when you're actually within'. Others were disparaging of the prevalence of firm mottoes and sayings that were intended to reinforce the striving, pressured or achieving image of Firm A staff:

> "the whole perception that you have to 'work hard' all the time and I don't think that's true really" (Audit Trainee, 1st Year).

> "When you go to the training courses they play Simply the Best to you at the start ... We got a talk at the start and they said 'We're sure you will succeed because we're chosen you, and we choose simply the best. We only choose the best people to do the best'. As far as I'm concerned that's silly because I don't know anybody that's joined this year who had a First for a start. So academically we're definitely not the best" (Audit Trainee, 1st Year).

This polarity that we observed in the reaction to the image of Firm A and its 'type' seemed to converge in the recognition that being a Firm A type: self-confident, hard working, professionally competent, perhaps arrogant or even loud, was only acceptable at higher levels of the organization. It may be significant that both of the above critical comments upon aspects of the firm's culture by design were from trainees in their first year. As one second year trainee put it, there was a wider perception that being 'loud', arrogant, etc. was acceptable behaviour once qualified but that "at [trainee] level you find it's more a question of be seen and not heard, if you're seen to be outgoing and sociable you're almost put down for it ...". For trainees, much of the image of being a Firm A type might be for external consumption only, whilst only at higher levels in the firm could the demonstrativeness associated with the firm type be expressed without offending immediate superiors and colleagues.

To what extent the 'culture of culture' within Firm A offers different training and socialization practices and experiences, the nature of our largely interview based research can offer only limited understandings. (In the succeeding section we consider the characteristics of Firm A and Firm B together to draw out some of the similarities and differences more explicitly.) It was noted by many of our interviewees that in Firm A there was monetary remuneration for overtime allowed for unqualified staff, in Firm B overtime was repaid through time off *in lieu*. Moreover, a number of trainees offered employment contracts by Firm A and other Big Six firms remarked that Firm A paid higher salaries to trainees. This higher payment might itself structure the 'type' (if there is a type) of Firm A employee since it might be taken to represent on the one hand the firm's 'extra' commitment to its staff whilst, on the other hand, appealing to the competitive instincts seen to be part of the Firm A ethos. It was also asserted by some of our respondents that Firm A placed great emphasis upon finishing audits within a shorter time period than other firms. Another consequence that doubtless connects to Firm A's cultural identity is that trainees claim to take on higher responsibilities, such as being in-charge of audits, at an earlier stage of their training than in other firms. Whether this is correct could only be gauged through measurement studies that we were unable to carry out but the idea that the cultural emphasis is connected to some differences in working practices seems plausible.

3.2 Professional Organization and Commercial Identity: The Leaders of Firm B

Firm B has not *actively* developed a distinct notion of its cultural or organizational identity. This is not at all to say that Firm B did not have a culture, but rather that its culture was not centrally concerned with conceptualizing *in terms of* having a culture - what we have called the 'culture of culture' in Firm A did not exist. We nevertheless found considerable evidence of corporate culture initiatives. For example, in the literature of Firm B, and in the appraisal and monitoring procedures that trainees were subject to, an emphasis upon the development of business skills and commercial orientations towards the client was a key feature. This is not to say that such issues were not important in Firm A also but that in the latter business awareness was subsumed by the more generalised collective work ethos. In Firm B recruitment and in-house training documents celebrated the idea that Firm B staff were Leaders in their fields; a re-working of the 'Simply the Best' motto of Firm A but which placed more stress upon the individual skills of staff rather than their collective identities as, say, Firm B 'types': a collective of leaders perhaps seems incongruous. In this sense staff in Firm B had not only a much less distinct organizational culture than Firm A (unsurprisingly) but did not regard the organization's self-image as an issue or problem. The orientation of the Firm B 'culture' was therefore seemingly more individualistic. It should be said at this point that part of the way in which Firm B's culture was defined by the trainees was in contra-distinction to their understandings of Firm A. Similarly, Firm A's culture is in part defined in opposition to other accountancy practices. In this sense, the two research sites are not 'independent', and the 'individualism' of Firm B is in part a reflection of a series of competitive standings between rival Big Six firms which impact upon the identity of individual trainees.

In part, the 'individualism' of Firm B is reflected or reinforced by several organizational characteristics of the practice. First, in the regional office of Firm B to which we gained access, audit staff were split into different client groupings: small business, public sector, etc. The fixing of audit trainees into such departments seemed to put the allegiances of the trainees to this group: reference was more often made to the advantages/disadvantages, equities/inequities between these groups than between say audit and tax divisions or departments. The issue of salary seemed to be a source of discontent amongst Firm B trainees generally but also between these sub-groups. It was also the case that members of the Tax department were not required to do the Chartered Accountancy examinations, and in one sub-group trainees were chosen to study for the Chartered Institute of Public Finance (CIPFA) examinations rather than ICAEW (again, full details of the internal structures of Firm B will be found in the following chapter).

Second, the organizational structures of Firm B were said to be less centralised than in Firm A; less of the discourse of Firm B was concerned to represent Firm B as 'national' or 'international' in character, although, as with all Big Six firms, plainly there is an international network of offices and employees signalling some commitment to the concept of 'one firm'. Nevertheless, in Firm B the regional office had, for example, much more autonomy in the personnel management (or HRM) initiatives that it was able to enact, although this might reflect the low status given to personnel functions within the firm (or Big Six firms generally; cf. Dirsmith *et al*, 1997). Indeed, if Firm A exhibited many of the characteristics associated with culture management techniques, Firm B seemed to be far more heavily influenced by the discourses of 'human resource management' (Legge, 1995). In particular, the use of competencies based appraisal systems, and the linkage of the competencies system into recruitment bears all the hallmarks of the integration of personnel issues into corporate strategy which is the claimed hallmark of human resource management.   Thus despite the apparently 'cultureless' and individualistic ethos of Firm B, techniques whose primary mode of operating is collective were much in evidence, and in this sense the language of 'new wave management' (Wood, 1989), if not of culture management *per se* was as much, if not more, a feature of Firm B as Firm A (see Anderson *et al*, 1996, for more detail on the status of human resource management in the two firms).

Each of these factors contributed towards the relative absence of a distinctive sense of the firm having a 'culture' amongst the trainees in Firm B. This is not to say there were not distinctive organizational characteristics to Firm B and we have tried to elaborate some of those. Nor is this to suggest that the view of the firm as more competitive or superior was not also present among trainees. Nevertheless, respondents to Firm B were more likely to see their firm as largely 'typical' of a Big Six practice rather than substantively different to the other firms.

Conclusion

Although we acknowledge and have attempted to clarify some of the differences in the socialization characteristics of Firm A and Firm B, we would wish to conclude with the summary of the commonalties between the firms with respect to the interrelationships between organizational and professional socialization:

- Professional and professionalism are commonly conceived in terms of conduct and behaviour rather than identity with an institution.
- Professional conduct is viewed as an art of impression management especially before the 'client', in whose name professional behaviour is often explained.
- Concepts of professional dress, conduct and language are identified with and mediated by the firm through formal appraisal mechanisms and through observation of the behaviour of peers.
- The discourse of professional generally emerges in contexts of criticism (of being unprofessional) rather than praise.

- The commitment of trainees to the professional qualification is dominated by the wider cultural view that it is a useful business credential for future careers outside of the firm.
- This instrumental view of professional accountancy training as a general business qualification undermines the concepts of the profession and professional transmitted by the firm.
- Firms lay great stress upon trainees passing their examinations and trainees experience the professional examinations as a process of 'getting through' rather than learning.
- A divergence of views exists on the relevance of the professional examinations to the content of everyday audit work: many see connections, many others do not.

6 Professional Socialization and Firm Divisionalization

Introduction

The third thesis which we set out to explore was that:

Socialization processes vary between divisions and give rise to differing conceptions of the role of the professional accountant

The background to this thesis was the recognition that CA practices have in recent years diversified considerably, and therefore different functional specialisms have arisen which might yield differing professional identities. However, in practice, we found such specialism has relatively little impact upon the trainees in this study, for whom the main relevant functional specialisms are those of Audit and Tax, since it is very unusual for trainees to work outside these divisions. The main exception to this was in Firm A, where some trainees were employed in the Insolvency division. Within our interview programme, only one trainee in either firm was identified as working in any of the more specialised consulting activities, and this individual was not registered for ICAEW examination.

In the light of this, the main issue which will be discussed in this chapter is that of the variation between trainees in Audit and Tax divisions. However, we also report on other subcultural differences which were identified by the research and comment on their relevance for professional socialization issues.

1. Audit and Tax

In general terms, the research suggested that the differences in sub-culture between Audit and Tax divisions within each firm were less significant than the differences in organizational culture between the two firms. We also found that the nature of the differences between Audit and Tax divisions themselves varied somewhat between the two firms.

1.1 Training and Accreditation

Trainees in the Audit and Tax divisions of Firm A are all registered for ICAEW examination (as are those in Insolvency). In this sense, the profession with which they might, in principle, identify is the same regardless of their divisional affiliation. Notwithstanding this, in practice both the nature of their work and the social norms obtaining within each division vary.

In Firm A, one of the key early socialization experiences, as noted in earlier chapters of this book, is that of the first residential training course undertaken by the trainees. Since these are in different locations, and have a different syllabus, for the two divisions, it follows that the possibilities for sub-cultural formation across divisions are limited, and this separation is re-inforced by much of the continuing pattern of training:

> "You're [together] when you do Institute exams, everyone's together, but for the rest of the time it's a very separate course" (Audit Trainee, 2nd Year).

Even when members of different divisions happen to be at the same training site, they tend to be separate. One trainee reported that on those occasions divisions:

> " ... didn't mix ... they (Tax) ate in a separate room" (Audit Trainee, 1st Year).

Of course what this reflects is the different types of work undertaken within the different divisions, and it is this in particular which sustains distinctive socialization processes, as will be examined shortly.

For Tax trainees, the process of professional training and accreditation is perceived as less directly related to their daily work than is the case for Audit. It is certainly true that Audit trainees sometimes complain about the lack of relevance of the syllabus and examination to their practical experience, but although the 'fit' may be disputed, it remains the case that, in principle, ICAEW examination stands in a direct relationship to auditing practice. At least for Tax trainees, the reported perception is that ICAEW examination is essentially designed for auditors:

> "[Most people] think Accountants - Audit. That may be the mark of the profession or the firm in general" (Tax Trainee, 3rd Year).

For such trainees, qualification is necessary in career terms but does not represent entrance into the accounting profession in so far as this is seen as the profession to which auditors belong. In this sense, professional identification within the Tax division is weaker than in Audit, although, as outlined elsewhere in this report, such identification is not especially marked even in Audit.

The differences between Audit and Tax in Firm B in terms of training and accreditation are more marked than in Firm A in that the majority of trainees in Firm B's Tax division are not registered for ICAEW examination. Instead, most trainees are registered for ATII examinations, and therefore professional identification with the accounting profession *per se* is more limited. Effectively, this marks a more developed version of the distinction already identified in Firm A between tax work and the accounting profession. However, the effect of the different qualifications for which audit and tax trainees are working in Firm B leads to perceived differences in status:

"I suppose it does seem as though theirs [i.e. ICAEW trainees'] is more important than our qualifications. I suppose they do get looked after a bit more than we do" (Tax Trainee, 2nd Year).

Whilst there may be status differences of this sort, they do at least mean that within Firm B there is less of the acrimony which was very strongly evident in Firm A with respect to the different conditions under which ICAEW study has to be undertaken. Whilst the details of these differences will be considered shortly, the general perception is that those in Audit divisions have a much more difficult task than those in Tax (and Insolvency). The assumption is that the more regular hours in Tax, and especially the fact that Tax trainees rarely have to go to work on Saturdays, creates inequitable conditions for studying:

"... we all have to sit the exams together and when they look at the exam results they will compare us equally but the people in Tax and Insolvency get more time off than us ..." (Audit Trainee, 3rd Year).

This is seen as particularly problematic in the context of competition between trainees and differential reward structures. As another Firm A Audit trainee complained:

"I came third equal with someone in Insolvency and I thought 'well he should beat me because he has more time than me', and one of the Tax people failed so I'm thinking like 'Hold on, he's got all these days off and he fails?' Strange, and he's paid, a thousand more a year?'" (Audit Trainee, 3rd Year).

Although these claims, coming as they do from Audit trainees, might be regarded simply as 'sour grapes', trainees in Tax acknowledge that their situation is easier in this respect, and cite it as one of the advantages of their specialism, whilst pointing out that they suffer as compared with their Audit colleagues by virtue of their lack of practical experience of much of the syllabus (nor can they accumulate the expenses audit trainees receive for travel mileage to clients, etc.). The difficulties here relate particularly to the end loaded or split intensive training modes (discussed in more detail later). These modes seemed to be designed in part to accommodate the audit busy season which falls between the two courses in this training mode. Since Tax trainees are not generally affected by the busy season, they have more time for study between the courses.

1.2 Organization of Work

The differences between Audit and Tax are not simply a feature of the difference in the technical practices of the work performed but also, relatedly, the way in which work is organised. Audit work typically requires trainees to be out of the office on client premises, often for a period of a week or two weeks, and sometimes longer:

> "There is quite a division. Just in the fact that if you work in Audit I suppose 90% of the time you're not physically in the office and you're at a client's on a long term basis" (Tax Trainee, 1st Year).

Almost all trainees in both firms identified this as the principal divisional difference. One consequence of this is that the audit team acts as a social reference point, as does the client, especially when trainees return in successive years to the same client. In Tax, work is more often confined to office hours and, for trainees especially, is more often on firm premises than on client premises. Moreover, a Tax trainee may well work on several clients in the course of a day rather than working exclusively for one client over a period of days (in Insolvency, relationship with clients may be even closer and more sustained than in Audit). This means that there is a greater possibility of identification with the division as a whole in Tax:

> "We are very team [meaning division] based in Tax ... we're all there all the time so I can just pop round to see somebody and discuss an issue" (Tax Trainee, 2nd Year).

Even in Tax this divisional unity may be mitigated by the fact that some trainees work primarily to one or two managers, but it remains the case that Tax is quite different to Audit, since Audit trainees when on client premises will have contact with a much smaller set of colleagues.

The consequences of this different pattern of working are manifest in a variety of ways.   Most obviously, they have consequences for the 'architecture' of work:

> "Tax [trainees are] more frequently in the office so you have your own desk, you've got your own computer and you do your own work ... as opposed to Audit where you don't have your own desk. You just have a little case and carry it around" (Audit Trainee, 2nd Year).

This also carries through into the way in which a trainee will organize his or her day in terms of work patterns. On an audit, trainees will have relatively prescribed activities, whereas in Tax:

> "We are very much left to our own devices ... I've kept my day filled with things I know I should be doing ... people don't tell you what to do" (Tax Trainee, 3rd Year).

1.2.1 Divisional Type There are perceptions of distinctive divisional 'type' or stereotype. For Audit trainees, this type is gregarious, business oriented and hardworking. For Tax trainees, the type is portrayed as more intellectual and analytical. That is not of course to say that trainees conform to such types, nor that they are mutually exclusive, but the different ways in which trainees describe the divisions does gesture towards an understanding of the differences between them, albeit expressed in stereotypical terms.

This stereotyping takes the form of fairly affable rivalry or competition so that:

> "We [Tax] think they [Audit] do nothing but go out and count numbers of stock and they think we do nothing but sit on our arses and just work a few figures out" (Tax Trainee, 1st Year).

This contrast is often played out through office humour, as described by an Audit trainee:

> "There's a sort of winding each other up about how boring each other's jobs are" (Audit Trainee, 1st Year).

A similar picture obtains in Firm B, although there are complicating factors there which will be discussed later. The present point is that divisional identities are confirmed through a stereotyping of sub-cultural differences. This implies not just that the divisions are differently structured but that the trainees value these structures differently. Thus the good points claimed for Audit by auditors - travel, variety, client contact - are portrayed negatively by Tax trainees as irregular hours, lack of stimulus, superficiality. Conversely, the Tax trainees represent stability and order as virtues whereas their Audit counterparts see these as evidence of the boring, routine nature of Tax work. The research did not yield any cases of trainees in one division seeing another division as a preferable place to work (although, as noted earlier, some saw advantages to Tax trainees in terms of time for study).

There are undoubtedly some quite complex processes of group and identity formation occurring here. To some extent, it may be the case that trainees have chosen their specialisms in line with their own preferences, formed prior to joining the firms. However, we would tend to doubt this on the basis that the degree to which applicants have any authentic knowledge of the type of work they will undertake is limited. It may also be that trainees are selected by the firms for different specialisms on the basis of an assessment of the suitability of individuals for the different types of work. Whilst there is certainly an attempt to do this, it is unlikely that it would be universally successful. It is more likely that the trainees acquire and sustain an identity through espousing the values of the group to which they happen to belong. Support for this conclusion comes from the nature of the social interactions which occur within the firms which we consider in the next section.

1.2.2 Social Life There are differences in the type of social life and interaction of trainees. In Audit, Friday night, particularly at the end of jobs, is a significant social event. This may be an event for the audit team only, but, typically, trainees will return to the office and socialize with others in the division. In Tax, there is a greater possibility of socializing during the week, at the end of the working day, although Friday night remains the most popular night. Tax trainees are, however, also much more likely to be able to socialise with each other at lunchtimes, and are more likely to socialize across the division as opposed to the team based socializing which can occur in Audit.

In both divisions, social life tends to decline in volume as time goes by because of the pressure of work and exam study. This particularly affects Audit, for two reasons. First, as noted earlier, the amount of non-work time available for private study is more restricted than for Tax trainees. Second, the demands of working away come to have an ever greater effect:

"... in the early days we used to go out every Friday and every Saturday together but as work pressures have built up ... we've become more fragmented. Because we were all together at one stage so it was quite easy to organize a night out, now people in Audit, you might have someone in London one day, Middlesbrough the next..." (Audit Trainee, 2nd Year).

This fragmentation again shows how the team is more likely to be a focus than the division, and this in turn implies a shifting social group insofar as the team for successive audit jobs is likely to be different.

The research showed a degree of variability between individuals and firms as to the extent of socializing between divisions. At the extreme:

"No. We [Audit and Tax] don't mix at all. We don't get much chance. After ... the first two weeks you don't see them again really" (Audit Trainee, 2nd Year).

In general, this sentiment was more common within Firm B than Firm A. Trainees reported seeing particular individuals from other divisions, but generally the pattern of segregation was confirmed. Clearly there are many factors which might over-ride this situation. For example, it is common for trainees to share homes with their colleagues, sometimes as a consequence of social relationships formed at university, and where these involve members of different divisions this inevitably has an effect on the degree of social contact. By the same token, for some trainees social life is not connected with work at all, especially where individuals are working in their home town or the town where they attended university.

1.2.3 Dress Codes There are some differences in dress and appearance codes for trainees between divisions. The main issue here is that dress codes in Tax are slightly more relaxed because face-to-face client contact is less than in Audit. This also links in to the issue of the divisional 'type' in that more relaxed dress codes may be a proxy for self-perception as being an intellectually oriented technical specialist rather than a business adviser. However, the distinctions here are relatively minor and should not be overstated.

1.2.4 Time-Keeping The different modes of client contact between Audit and Tax mean that time-keeping issues are very distinct. In order to allow charging calculations to be made, it is necessary that Tax trainees keep an accurate record of the clients on which they have been working during the day. For example, if, whilst working on one client, a phone call is taken from another client, it is necessary to record this so that charges can be allocated accordingly. Trainees typically begin their day by completing time records for the previous day, although there is some variation in the practices of individuals in this respect. For Audit trainees, time-keeping is normally more straightforward since they are working on one client for a block of time. There was also some evidence that in Tax the possibility of slightly more flexibility in working arrangement was possible; for example, arriving at the office late but then working late, and *vice versa*. In Audit the 'presentation to client' imperative that seems to structure much of the behaviour of Audit trainees would deem arriving late unacceptable even if it were to be compensated by working late.

In Firm B, there were several reports that the pressures to complete an audit job within budget (i.e. using the specified amount of staff time) led to pressure for unpaid overtime from trainees. As we noted in Chapter 4 for those trainees who were near-qualified not recording all the hours worked at a particular client was taken as an important symbol of organizational commitment and was deemed to enhance career prospects within the firm. Such practices were also reported to be common amongst the audit managers but we found no evidence of this in Tax divisions.

1.2.5 Appraisal Finally, trainees in Audit and Tax are appraised differently. Thus:

> "People [in Audit] work on a job for two weeks and then will get feedback on their performance on that job ... so they could get two ratings a month ... whereas we, the aim is to have one every three months whereas in fairness it's probably every six months. Or even longer than that" (Tax Trainee, 2nd Year).

The same situation obtained in Firm B:

> "For the Auditors it is very clear cut because you go on an audit for two weeks. You get a job review form ... so they would do one for every job..." (Tax Trainee, 1st Year).

The significance of this difference is difficult to assess. First, the periods specified for formal appraisal of trainees were not always adhered to in Audit, and job review forms, as we have noted, were often very late. Second, given the questions raised about the utility of appraisal (reported elsewhere in this book) it might be suggested that Tax trainees are fortunate in this respect. However, from the point of view of professional and organizational socialization, the difference could be significant. Insofar as appraisal socializes trainees through the evaluation and correction of their conduct, it might be that Tax trainees are relatively unsocialized. But, at the same time, it may be that informal appraisal becomes more significant within Tax. This remains an open question.

2. Other Forms of Sub-Culture

Although the thesis focused on divisional differences, it must be recognized that this gives privilege to only one aspect of formal organizational structure. In fact, the research revealed a range of other distinctions within both of the firms which had some significance, and which, to some degree, cut across the Tax-Audit distinctions reported above.

2.1 Year Group

There are clear indications that the year group is a significant reference point for most trainees, and this implies also that it acts as an arena for socialization. In both firms, trainees usually join the firm *en masse* at the same time (late Summer), although in some cases they may have had prior experience within the firm in a 'scholar' capacity. The research suggested that year group was of greater significance in Firm A than in Firm B, because year structures are more rigid in Firm A (continuing after qualification, for example), whilst the greater variety of qualifications studied for in Firm B has the effect of fracturing year group solidarity.

As with divisions, the extent of socializing is an indicator of the significance of the group, and by that yardstick the significance of the year group does tend to decline over time:

> "Years tend to socialize together because you go through training together and that's who your strongest bonds are with and so most years go out with each other. Every so often you will get someone from the year above or the year below out with you but obviously the further away in terms of rank someone gets the less likelihood there is of socializing with them" (Audit Trainee, 2nd Year).

This is not just a reflection of the general trend to less out-of-work contact in Audit identified above, for the same phenomenon occurs in Tax:

> "At the beginning when you first start at the Firm [my] year were all together in a room every day for three weeks so you bond very much as a year, just your

intake [later] you come into [a division] and gradually you get in on that. I very rarely go out with the people in my year now" (Tax Trainee, 3ʳᵈ Year).

This shift from year group to divisional identification appears to occur during the first two years within the firm. In any case, there was evidence of considerable variations in the significance of the year group according to circumstances, which will be briefly described.

2.1.1 Exempt/Non-Exempt   The most important fracture within any year group in both firms is between those trainees who, by virtue of previous experience or training (usually because they are 'relevant' graduates) have some exemption:

> "They split the year into two [exempt and non-exempt]" (Audit Trainee, 1ˢᵗ Year).

In particular, the extent to which a year group is split between those undertaking General Conversion Course (GCC) and those who are exempt is important. Since this split will vary between different year groups, it follows that the extent of year group solidarity will vary. GCC appears to function as an important first introduction to trainees' professional careers:

> "We've [i.e. GCC exempt] met people since we came back [from clients] but we haven't had that initial bond at the beginning which would have been quite useful" (Tax Trainee, 1ˢᵗ Year).

This is an interesting quotation. It gestures towards the perceived significance of GCC and the impact of exclusion from it, but it also suggests how readily trainees will seek or assume group identity - for this trainee, exempt students are constituted as "we". That group identities do form in this way was widely confirmed by the trainees:

> "... there were half of us who did conversion straight away and half who didn't ... so we became quite close knit and they became quite close knit..." (Audit Trainee, 1ˢᵗ Year).

It seems that this split can have an enduring significance:

> "... the people who were relevant graduates were alienated to begin with because everybody else was on this full-time course ... I know a couple of the relevant

graduates did have trouble fitting in and still do to an extent" (Audit Trainee, 2ⁿᵈ Year).

In addition to potential problems of fitting in, relevant graduates felt that they suffered in the early part of their training in having to do more 'ticking and bashing' than their non-exempt counterparts. They also felt that too much was expected of their prior qualifications, pointing out that the knowledge they had gained at degree level was largely 'theoretical'.

2.1.2 Training Mode and Training Firm Within both firms, different training modes were employed. These modes were:

- Link (Firm B only): A combination of days of study leave, courses and home study.
- End-Loaded ('Split Intensive' in Firm A):
  An initial short full-time course, followed up with self-learning study packs with a longer (nine week) course prior to examination (Firm B), or two separate eight week blocks (Firm A).
- Full-Time: A 12 week course (16 weeks in Firm A) immediately followed by examination.

Different modes might be used at different stages of training. Courses were provided by external tutors. Firm A used one tutor only, whereas Firm B used a different tutor largely according to which training mode was being used.

Inevitably different training modes led to trainees having an involvement with different groups, particularly at external tutors. Clearly on both End-Loaded and Full-Time modes these groups are potentially significant sites of socialization since long periods of time will be spent within the group.

We found some evidence that training mode is not an arbitrary matter and carries a degree of symbolic significance. Although, especially in Firm B, there was some suggestion that trainees could choose their training mode (if they were prepared to pay for one particular tutoring firm), the reality in both firms was that trainees were allocated to a particular mode. Many trainees believe that only stronger trainees are offered the Full-Time mode, and so status differentials and, perhaps, career prospects are linked into training mode:

"It was really definitely a split according to ability like all the ones who did best in the conversion course went through and did it full time and then the second group did split intensive. The weaker ones I guess" (Audit Trainee, 2ⁿᵈ Year).

In terms of the earlier distinctions amongst trainees, training mode groups formed a sub-set of the year group whilst potentially cutting across divisions. In addition, it should be noted that within Firm B, the distinction of relevant and non-relevant graduates is compounded by the fact that, even when on the same training mode, they will be sent to different tutorial firms.

2.2 Firm B: Departmental Structure

In the earlier discussion of the Tax-Audit distinction, we put to one side distinctions within the divisions themselves. In fact, in both divisions of both firms there were sub-groups and specialisms within divisions, of which by far the most significant was the departmental structure within the Audit division of Firm B. As we noted in the previous chapter, these departments are structured around particular client groups, either reflecting particular business sectors (e.g. 'Leisure') or the size of clients. This *could* have considerable implications for the experience of trainees. For example, in a group dealing with large clients it would be likely that year-ends will be bunched leading to a peak of work activity. In small client departments, year-ends tended to be more staggered and therefore the work will be more regular. On the other hand, the extent of guidance needed by clients from larger concerns will be less, and typically contact between client and auditors - especially trainees - will be at a lower level.

In Firm B, trainees will normally only be moved between departments if needed, and this means that trainees' socialization experiences even within the Audit division may vary considerably:

> "Each department in the office has got a very distinct personality.... Just very subtle little changes but you think you could be working in a completely different firm" (Audit Trainee, 3rd Year).

This departmental structure did not have a counterpart in Firm A. There are some tax specialisms, but these were not reported as especially significant. Within Audit, although it might be that managers or Partners might specialise in particular types of client, trainees would normally work across the whole client range. That said, the client base of Firm A, in so far as it can be generalized, was less varied in terms of size than for Firm B.

2.3 Firm A: Insolvency Division

As mentioned at the beginning of this chapter, one of the main distinguishing factors between Firm A and B is the fact that Firm A takes trainees directly into an Insolvency division. Whilst these trainees are ICAEW students, they have different modes of working to both Audit and Tax, and they express a different understanding of 'divisional type'.

Insolvency trainees differ from Tax trainees in that they will spend a considerable amount of time out of the office on client premises. However, unlike Audit trainees, their contact with clients will be more sustained than the one or two weeks normally spent on an audit, potentially stretching over several months or even years. They are also likely to be involved in a greater range of activities, including those relating to the management of bankrupt firms, although in another sense their experience is more limited than Audit trainees since, by definition, the clients they see are likely to be insolvent or experiencing other major problems. The experience of Insolvency trainees is described as being exhilarating, responsible and varied:

> " ... in Insolvency you don't necessarily know what you are doing from one day to the next ... you are actually 22 years old and you're going into a shop and you are actually asking to speak to the manager ... you are a representative of the Receiver and basically you are telling him that the wheels have come off the wagon ..." (Insolvency Trainee, 2nd Year).

This leads to a rather different set of perceived characteristics. The Insolvency 'type' is likely to be seen as needing stronger interpersonal and business skills, given the range of people that have to be dealt with and the sometimes sensitive tasks that must be performed, especially in relation to the workforce of insolvent companies.

3. Professional and Organizational Socialization

Our primary interest in the divisional and other sub-cultural differences which we have outlined relates to their impact upon conceptions of professional and organizational identity. Given the distinction between, in particular, Audit and Tax it is reasonable to infer that these identities differ somewhat: Audit and Tax trainees define themselves differently and, what is more, do so explicitly by reference to each other. On the issue of professional socialization, it is clear that the different qualifications pursued within Firm B entail a clear demarcation of professional reference groups, and within both firms we found some indication that ICAEW accreditation is seen primarily as an Auditors qualification. But in any case, as reported elsewhere, we found identity with the accounting profession to be weak and, therefore, for both Audit and Tax trainees ICAEW qualification is seen primarily in terms of its capacity to offer a career-enhancing qualification. Professional identity refers more to behavioural attributes than anything else. This representation obtained across divisions. Given this, it is appropriate to consider divisional differences as they relate to careers and to professional behaviour. Attention will then be given to organizational socialization issues.

As regards careers, we found that Audit was seen as having the strongest capacity to offer a general, transferable business training. Tax is perceived to be a rather narrower specialism. Some trainees (in both divisions) claimed that it was easier to gain entry to Tax than Audit in terms of the number of applications for the respective divisions and in that sense offered an 'easier' route in, whilst offering more restricted opportunities on qualification. The main reason for the latter perception was that Audit was seen as a preparation for finance and accounting careers within the commercial sector. At issue here is not just the experience of auditing but also the fact that clients might become future employers. In Firm A, Insolvency was also seen as offering strong prospects for future employment because of the range of business skills which it involves.

A crucial concept in trainees' accounts of the career value of professional qualification was that of being 'rounded'. This refers to having a breadth of experiences and skills. In this regard, the Audit trainee was considered to be more rounded than the Tax trainee, and in Firm A Insolvency trainees were seen by themselves as being more rounded still, although we did not find this perception of Insolvency being held by trainees in Audit or Tax. In Firm B, trainees were less likely to be as rounded as in Firm A because the departmental structure often limited their experience.

Whilst all divisions of both firms stressed the behavioural aspects of professionalism, there was some variation in what this meant. For Audit trainees, the capacity to present well face-to-face was slightly more important than in tax, where direct client contact is more limited. In Tax, the ability to present well on the telephone and on paper was more important, although this was also an issue for Audit trainees to a slightly lesser extent. In Insolvency, professional behaviour loomed largest, and this seems to be for two reasons. First, the situations an Insolvency trainee faces are more likely to be 'delicate' and to require personal skills. Insofar as, for trainees, Audit and Tax work is more routine and less contentious there was less call for these skills. Secondly, the nature of the technical knowledge required by Insolvency work is perhaps less precise than for Audit and Tax trainees in that it might relate to more judgmental and managerial issues. Thus, again, personal credibility is at the fore and professional behaviour in dress and manner is seen as helping to bestow this credibility.

Finally, we consider the implications of sub-cultural differences for organizational socialization. It is plain that the vehicles or arenas of organizational socialization for the trainee are likely to be the smaller groups which he or she experiences. Thus organizational values will be transmitted through divisions, audit teams, tutor groups and so on. Thus the differences outlined in this chapter might be expected to have some impact on the nature and extent of organizational socialization. However, as reported elsewhere, we found relatively strong organizational cultures, especially in Firm A, and this leads us to conclude that the differences within the firms were less strong than the differences between firms. The experience of Audit in Firm A was notably different to Audit in Firm B, for example. This can be related to the nature of the client base, the departmental structure in Firm B and, perhaps most important to the trainee, the higher levels of overtime required in Firm A. The Tax divisions in the two firms were also markedly different in terms of the variety of professional qualifications for which students studied.

By comparison with these differences, the distinctions between divisions *within* firms appear relatively minor, even though the work and work structure vary considerably, as reported. It is likely that a trainee could move divisions within a firm, and still 'fit in', much more easily than s/he could move between firms. This is difficult to demonstrate since in practice such moves are rare, although in Firm A some trainees have moved successfully from Audit to Insolvency. There was one interviewee in Firm B who had previously worked for Firm A, and he reported the organizational experiences as being drastically different, confirming our view on this.

Conclusion

- There are distinctive Audit and Tax sub-cultures, expressed in terms of:
  - examination
  - exam study experiences
  - client contact/ office time
  - divisional type
  - social life
  - appraisal experiences
- Year group is a significant reference point, but one which declines in significance over time.

- The split between Exempt and non-Exempt students constitutes a major fissure of the year group.
- Training mode and tutorial agency can yield different socialization groups.
- In general, divisional differences have limited impact on professional socialization.
- In general, divisional differences are less important than organizational differences.

7 Conclusion

Introduction

The professions play a central role in the economies and societies of the modern world, and, as such, they have commanded considerable academic attention. One of the central issues in the functioning and maintenance of any profession is the way in which it enrols individuals and 'makes' them into professionals. The nature of this process will have important implications for the ability of a profession to attract clients as well as to establish its wider position in society. There exists a large and well-established body of research which shows that the process of becoming a professional involves much more than simply passing examinations and being registered to practice. Rather, becoming a professional is a complex *accomplishment* which involves induction into a wide array of formal and informal norms which have to be both taught and learned, whether consciously or not. This process is one of *socialization*.

Whilst it is true that the professions have attracted considerable attention, it remains the case that accountancy has been relatively neglected compared with, in particular, medicine and law. Certainly in relation to, specifically, socialization processes very few studies of accountants have been made. The research presented in this book was aimed towards rectifying this omission, whilst drawing upon such previous work as exists in order to illuminate this important aspect of the study of the professions. The results should be of interest not just to academics working in the field but also to practitioners and policy-makers. The research, whilst certainly having limitations in terms of size and scope which we will discuss later, is believed to be the largest and most detailed qualitative study of professional socialization of trainee chartered accountants conducted in the UK.

Professional socialization in accountancy (and in many other professions) cannot be separated from processes of organizational socialization. ICAEW trainees are employed by particular organizations which, on the one hand, are a principal arena in which professional socialization occurs whilst, on the other hand, like any other organization have there own formal and informal norms into which new recruits are socialized. The research was designed to explore both the general issue of professional socialization and the organizationally specific contexts in which it occurs. We therefore structured the research around three central theses:

Thesis 1: *Socialization processes focus not only upon examination performance, but presentation to clients and ability to integrate with the social norms of peers, managers and partners.*

Thesis 2: *The socialization of trainees is into organizational culture first and professional culture second.*

Thesis 3: *Socialization processes vary between divisions and give rise to differing conceptions of the role of the professional accountant.*

These theses have in turn been used to structure the presentation in this book of the empirical findings of the research. However, this empirical research was itself located in a thorough review of existing literature on the professions and sought to engage with the arguments presented within the literature, especially that research concerned with socialization in the process of professionalization.

1. Literature and Methodology

In *Chapter 2*, therefore, we presented a detailed overview of past studies of the professions. We noted in particular the fragmentation of approaches to the study of professions, considering Marxist, Weberian, Functionalist, Trait and Symbolic Interactionist perspectives. Within this latter perspective, in particular, issues of professional behaviour are of central importance (Becker *et al*, 1961; Dingwall, 1979). Without necessarily subscribing to all of the theoretical commitments of Symbolic Interactionism, we do concur with what seems to be the current consensus in the literature on the importance of professional behaviour to the constitution of professions. This seems to be justified by our consideration of such literature as exists specifically on the socialization of trainee accountants (Harper, 1988; Power, 1991; Coffey, 1993) which all supports the claim that:

> "The minutiae of personal conduct and appearance might seem unimportant but in fact they are as crucial as the firm's procedures and proformas that guide an auditor through the daily work, or the process for the selection and training of staff. Great care is taken to get the right work performed, in the right way, by the right people, wearing the right clothes. Of such stuff is the garment of

professionalism made: and such is the display of knowledge and trustworthiness that justifies monopoly" (Macdonald, 1995, p.207).

The last sentence of this quotation points towards the wider context and significance of forms of professional behaviour. As stated earlier, professional socialization is important in the establishment and maintenance of the social and economic power of the accountancy profession. The earlier sections of Chapter 2 were therefore devoted to considering the context of the accounting profession and the nature of its professional claim. This included attention being given to the diversity of professional bodies within accountancy and the need for the accounting profession to maintain itself in the face of various types of criticism. Indeed, one of the most important modern studies of the nature of professions (Abbott, 1988) has shown how professions are always engaged in a ongoing process to legitimate themselves, to defend their professional 'jurisdiction' against outsiders and to extend the territory of this professional jurisdiction - perhaps at the expense of other professions - where possible.

By the conclusion of Chapter 2 we had established the complexity of the circumstances in which any study of accountants' professional socialization necessarily takes place. These circumstances include the institutional and organizational context in which accountants work, but also the sheer variety of issues to which the academic literature has drawn attention. In the face of this, it is obviously important to design research which is capable theoretically of apprehending these issues and their complexity, and which employs appropriate methods so to do.

In *Chapter 3* we outlined the methodological approach adopted in the study. Methodology is not the same as method in that the former refers to a set of wider philosophical and theoretical considerations which help to inform the choice of the latter. As regards the wider considerations, we drew a broad distinction between 'positivist' and 'phenomenological' or interpretative research traditions and indicated the reasons why this study is located in this second tradition. We then focused on the details of the research undertaken. At the centre of the research was a programme of 77 semi-structured interviews conducted at two Big Six firms (Firm A and Firm B). We explained the use of *The Ethnograph* software package in the analysis of the interview material and pointed to some of complexities and problems of using such software. One of the key points made in Chapter 3 is that phenomenological approaches to research do not yield simple conclusions which offer immediate recipes for practical application or prescription. Instead, the virtue of such research is its ability to speak adequately to the ambiguities and unintended consequences of social relations such as those involved in professional socialization.

2. Summary of Findings

Chapters 4, 5 and *6* provided the detailed results of the research organised around each of the three theses outlined above. Rather than summarise these findings sequentially, the remainder of this concluding chapter will be given over to drawing together the material presented in order to provide an overview of its main themes.

2.1 Processes of Socialization

The processes of professional socialization do not have a definite beginning and end. A university student applying for an accountancy training contract will already have undergone some form of relevant socialization in terms of the development of some understanding, however rudimentary, of what it means to be an accountant. In the case of students on an accountancy degree this socialization process may be rather more advanced or explicit. Our study only shed indirect light upon these early socialization experiences, although the importance of prior judgements by trainees that accountancy is a valuable general business qualification emerged as a key element in our analysis. However, we concentrated on socialization from the recruitment period onwards.

The study showed that this period can be extremely important in developing an early sense of what it means to be an accountant. Certainly in terms of organizational socialization, the recruitment period is one of the few occasions on which an individual is exposed to a number of different firms and makes judgements between them. Although the trainees to whom we spoke had limited contact with other firms *via* tutorial firms or at Institute social events, the bulk of their impression of firms other than the one they work for comes from the recruitment period. This is significant in terms of the formation of an organizational identity in that such identities are always formed not just through identification with the employing organization but also in contradistinction to other organizations. By the same token, the recruitment procedure is a significant part of the socialization process from the firm's point of view since it allows the exclusion of applicants who are deemed to be unlikely to 'fit in' with the organization.

We found that the firms studied differed in the nature of their recruitment processes. In Firm B formal techniques and measurements of selection were more strongly evident than in Firm A (although they were present to some extent in both firms). Irrespective of this, however, we found that the personal impression given by an applicant at interview, especially the impression given to Partners, could be significant in the decision to recruit regardless of the outcome of formal tests. Here we see the beginning of one of the main findings of the research: the importance of behaviour and 'impression management', which will be returned to shortly. We did not detect *major* differences in the types of qualities sought by the two firms either academically or personally, and many of the trainees interviewed had been offered contracts at more than one Big Six firm, implying some homogeneity in the standards applied. For trainees holding multiple offers, their impressions gained during recruitment determine their choice of firm.

Although organizational socialization issues are present in this way from an early stage, we did not find much evidence of a strong sense of professionalism being formed during recruitment, at least on the part of the trainees. Rather, we found that trainees arrived at the firms with only a limited sense of what the work of an accountant entailed, and then not always an accurate picture: many found that they had overstated the extent to which foreign travel and work variety were a feature of trainees' experience, and some felt that the firms had contributed to this misperception.

On joining a firm, trainees quickly become involved in a whole series of socialization processes. These include the formal structures of appraisal and training, and informal structures such as social contact and peer group. Whilst it is helpful to draw some distinction between these formal and informal processes, the reality is that they cannot always be readily separated. One of the key examples of this is appraisal. We found that appraisal mechanisms put a great stress upon the behaviour of trainees and their capacity to fit in with those around them. Although much of what is appraised is the technical performance on jobs, in practice this distinction is difficult to sustain because judgements about the technical are invariably subsumed into judgements about the person made in the context of social relationships between the appraiser and the appraisee. This is compounded by the fact that in both firms appraisals are often completed a long time after the work which they appraise. In these circumstances it is unsurprising that appraisal focuses on general impressions of the trainee and the reputation enjoyed by that individual.

Mentoring is a further example of a formal socialization process which also operates informally. Both firms had some formal mentoring procedures, although in Firm B these were much more elaborate and explicit. In both firms we found that much 'mentoring' occurred informally however. Thus trainees would form relationships with superiors who were particularly supportive and who would offer advice and assistance on a range of issues such as career development. In many cases these were quite outside the formal mentoring system, although there was considerable variation between individuals on this point. In some cases only lip service was paid to formal mentoring procedures. In other cases there was a convergence between the formal and the informal.

Just as appraisal and mentoring are only superficially formal rather than also being informal, so socializing is only superficially informal. We found that trainees' social life, especially in the early weeks of joining, is actively promoted by the firms. In some cases, training events are at least as much about this social aspect as about the their formal purposes. Socializing is an important part of the formation of peer groups which act as vehicles for the formation of organizational and professional values. We found very substantial evidence that peer groups in the firms are extremely fragmented. Although year group forms an initial focus in many cases, subsequently the importance of this group diminishes. Instead, we identified a series of cleavages between specialisms (especially Audit and Tax); between exempt and non-exempt trainees; between training modes. Moreover, irrespective of the type of peer group in question, we found a complex mixture of co-operation and competition within such groups. Whilst peer groups of trainees operated as a primary reference point and could offer mutual support over training issues, they were also sites of competition between trainees. In both firms we found that trainees had a sense of themselves as individuals in competition with each other for career and examination success.

2.2 Making Up Accountants: Defining the Professional

Having identified the main vehicles for socialization, we are now in a position to consider what values were transmitted, especially as regards those relating to professionalism. Notwithstanding organizational differences, we found that by far the dominant understanding of being a professional learnt by the trainees related to codes of *behaviour*. The significance of this should be stressed. It means that the trainees did not understand professional identity in terms of the possession of knowledge, nor in accreditation to practice, nor in terms of commitments to public service.

Professional behaviour had many aspects to it. The most obvious was that of appropriate dress and appearance generally (hair, make-up, jewellery etc.). In addition, behaving seriously and soberly was important. Time-keeping was also frequently mentioned, including the willingness to work overtime as and when necessary. For the trainees themselves, these were the meanings of being a professional. Although, as will be discussed shortly, trainees were concerned to pass examinations, few of them offered being qualified as part of their understanding of being a professional, still less did they articulate any sense of the ethical or public service aspects of professionalism, even when pressed to do so. This was true for almost all trainees interviewed in both firms and across different specialisms.

If trainees understand being a professional primarily in terms of behaviour, it is because this is what they have been taught in the socializing processes identified above. The firms themselves, the various sub-groups and peer groups we have mentioned and, we believe, the tutorial firms tend to reproduce this understanding of the professional. We found that the main method and rationale for this was that of the 'client' and 'service to the client'. It is felt that appropriate behaviours in terms of appearance, manner, presentation and self-conduct are a vital part of giving good client service and that failure in these respects may lead to loss of clients. Client service is elevated as perhaps the central value transmitted by socialization, to the extent that one trainee felt that such service should be provided even where it involved dishonest or morally dubious actions. However, what we did not find from the trainees was a sense of the fact that their client, as defined in successive Companies Acts, is the (often absent) owners rather than the (immediately present) managers of the company.

Client service was a central value, and, therefore, the pursuit of career success depended upon contributing to this, so that trainees are aware that one of the easiest routes to failure was to antagonize a client. For a trainee this would be most likely to occur through inappropriate behaviour, and the definition of such behaviour as 'unprofessional' was therefore important in the provision of client service and the achievement of career success. In other words, we found some evidence that the idea of being a professional was typically articulated in *negative* terms, that is, in terms of being *un*professional.

Although professional behaviour was most strongly linked to client service issues, we found that it was also important in relation to colleagues and superiors. The willingness to perform even mundane tasks enthusiastically and efficiently was seen as a form of professional behaviour and was also seen as a way of creating favourable impressions with superiors. Thus, again, impression management would seem to be at the heart of the trainees' conception of the meaning of being professional. We did find some variation on this issue as between different specialisms, with impression management, perhaps, looming larger for audit trainees than for tax trainees because the former had more face-to-face client contact.

As regards differences between the firms, on the issue of the conceptualistion of being a professional, we found very few differences. In both cases, behaviour in terms of appearance, manner and conduct were the dominant understandings of professionalism. This was true both when trainees gave spontaneous responses to questions about what was meant by being a professional and when we attempted to suggest to them other meanings of professionalism. However, we did find differences between the firms with respect to their organizational cultures. The main way we characterised this difference was in terms of the fact that Firm A had a 'culture of culture' - in other words, culture was the explicit object of design and discussion. In Firm B, although it 'had' a culture, and although there was some evidence of culture management, there was very little explicit invocation of culture, at least by the trainees. As a very rough distinction, it might be said that Firm A's culture was more collectivist and Firm B's more individualist, at least in terms of its discourse. Although the reality is rather more complex than this (trainees in both firms displayed a complex mix of co-operative and competitive behaviours), the key point for present purposes is that the distinctions of organizational culture did not significantly impact upon the question of the definition of professionalism. In both cases, the outcomes of socialization in terms of the focus on overt behaviour were similar.

2.3 Making Up Accountants: Credentialism and Career

If the dominant understanding of being a professional referred to behavioural attributes, it is pertinent to consider how the trainees understood processes of examination and qualification, given that these might have been expected to figure strongly in the trainees' account of being a professional. After all, leaving aside even public service issues, one of the commonest ways in which professions are defined is in terms of the fact that its members can prove that they possess a defined body of knowledge. In fact examination and qualification were extremely important to the trainees, but nevertheless did not normally form a substantial part of their accounts of being professional.

The primary rationalistion expressed by the trainees was that of gaining a qualification. The chartered accountancy qualification was widely perceived to offer a good general business qualification. The issue for trainees was 'getting' the qualification as a passport to wider career goals, which might often be outside the accountancy profession. In some cases, the choice of accountancy seemed to be little more than a matter of inertia carrying individuals from university to a training contract. For others, it offered a way of compensating for a commercially 'irrelevant' degree. And for others still, it represented the normal progression from having done a relevant accounting degree. As such, professional status was regarded as no different in type from other types of qualification (such as MBA) albeit that, by definition, the trainees to whom we spoke saw it as having advantages over the alternatives on offer. These advantages might include the fact that the qualification could be gained whilst earning a reasonable salary rather than having to both pay fees and forego earnings.

As we noted in *Chapter 2* the understanding that in the UK accountancy is a valuable and valued management qualification seems to be reflected in the relative proportions of accountants holding senior management positions in large companies. Although we found some evidence that trainees became committed to their training firms, we found very little indication of a commitment to the work itself, and still less did we find a moral commitment to accountancy *per se*. The dominant attitude towards the qualification was therefore what educational theorists have called *credentialism* - by which is meant the achievement of qualification as an end in itself or instrumentally as a means towards some other reward, rather than according the qualification an intrinsic value. In this way although professional socialization is largely defined by the organizational, these commitments seem to be undercut by the trainees apparent instrumentalist attitudes towards the training and qualification process. It seems to us plausible to see the relative lack of professional or organizational identity as an *unintended outcome* of the success that accountants in the UK have had in moving into areas of corporate management (and other organizations) that are not directly concerned with the practice of accounting or auditing. The absence of professionalism as a state of being is both a medium and outcome of the extensive and varied markets for accounting labour in the UK.

The value of accounting as a qualification also structured trainees' attitudes to examinations. These were widely seen as of central importance to the trainees' lives, but largely as an obstacle to be cleared. There was much less evidence of the content of examinations being seen as central. In effect, examinations became a trial of strength between the competing pressures which might make an individual fail. If the qualification was something to be 'got', examinations were something to be 'got through'. Although there were mixed views as to the relevance of the examinations to actual experience, with the prevailing view being that they were of limited relevance, the issue goes beyond this. In a sense, the trainees seemed to see the relevance of examinations as itself being irrelevant since, in any case, they needed to get through them in order to achieve the qualification. Unsurprisingly, given an attitude that moralists and others might call cynical, some trainees ascribed a similarly cynical motive to the ICAEW, seeing the examinations as primarily a mechanism for restricting entry. It might almost be said that the relationship between trainee and professional body was conflictual in that the latter was seen as erecting the 'barriers' which were at the same time the 'hurdles' which the trainees must jump. At the same time, contact with the institute was perceived as being limited to the collection of fees and the setting of examinations and regulations. Or as one trainee remarked, "You get a binder."

This instrumental attitude on the part of trainees again emerges, at least in part, as a result of the socialization processes we identified, although we suggest that wider social attitudes are important too. In particular, the way in which trainees come to sense that the external tutoring agencies focus upon examination technique serves to re-affirm the understanding of examinations as a hurdle to be jumped rather than having any intrinsic value as modes for imparting knowledge. In addition, within both of the firms trainees perceived that examinations and qualification were treated negatively - it was a problem if a trainee failed, whereas passing was more or less assumed. Certainly the biggest pressure the trainees need to cope with is that of the demands of overtime, and here we found some functional differences, with audit trainees experiencing worse time pressures than tax trainees because of overtime, travelling to clients and unpredictability of time demands.

From the point of view of trainees, the signal coming from their firms seemed to be one in which examination performance is not a strong feature of professional or organizational identity. Failing examinations will prevent continued employment, but professionalism was not explicitly understood in terms of examination success. Indeed we found some evidence that examination failure was treated more sympathetically, especially at GCC, if the individual concerned was seen in other respects as conforming to the norms of behaviour (so that whereas GCC failure normally led to sacking, this might be relaxed in some cases). Similarly, the impact on career prospects of having to re-sit examinations would vary according to perceptions of the individual concerned. At the same time, trainees perceive that firms often seem to give primary status to the demands of the client, both in terms of the issues of professional behaviour and in terms of overtime demands, and therefore this contributes to the general downgrading of examinations and qualification to the status of a necessary evil rather than a defining attribute of being a professional.

3. Reconsidering the Research Problematic

If we now return to the three guiding theses of the research we can give brief, albeit not straightforward, answers to the central questions.

We conclude that *Thesis 1* is justifiable. Presenting well to clients and successful integration with peers and superiors is *central* to socialization processes in both of the firms studied. Successful examination performance, whilst a necessary condition for the continuation of training and ultimately for accreditation is by no means a sufficient condition for the achievement of professional identity. Indeed, appropriate behaviour is the dominant understanding of the meaning of being a professional, whereas examinations are seen instrumentally as a vehicle to achieving a qualification which in turn is a vehicle to career success.

On *Thesis 2*, we are not able to give such a categorical answer. It is certainly the case that organizational socialization is primary in that it is at the level of the organization rather than the profession that socialization occurs. Moreover, trainees' awareness and understanding of 'profession' and 'professional' are largely negotiated by the organization, such that professional socialization is to a significant extent an outcome of their organizational socialization within the firms. However, given the processes of instrumentality and credentialism that we observed in the values of the trainees, it is not the case that they simply identify with the organization rather than the profession, or indeed with the profession *as constructed by* the practices of the organization, since the process seems to be that they identify much more strongly, at least during training, with a sense of their careers than with organization *or* profession. Where organizational commitment was found, it seems likely that this reflects cases where individuals see themselves as having a career within the organization, and in this sense embodies the same instrumentality. Moreover, although organizations may be the primary arena for professional socialization, the fact that the outcomes in both firms are so similar would tend to suggest that the processes at work are not organizationally specific in the way implied by Thesis 2. The main caveat we would add to this conclusion is that closer to qualification some trainees did re-assess their visions of 'career' in terms of a possible longer future with the firm.

We believe that the research demonstrates *Thesis 3* to be largely false. There are certainly differences in the type of socialization processes between different functional specialisms, and we identified several different peer groups at work within the firms. However, it was not the case that these gave rise to differing conceptions of the role of the professional accountant. This is because of the fact that, regardless of specialism, the dominant understanding of being a professional was in terms of behaviour - appearance, manner and conduct - and behavioural standards only showed minor variations between divisions. Similarly, the perception of examinations and qualifications was instrumental regardless of division.

4. Limitations of this Research and Further Work

Although we believe this study to have been the largest and most detailed of its sort, it is plain that it has limitations, some of which are inherent in work of this type. The most obvious limitation is that we have confined ourselves to Big Six firms. Whilst these are the major players in chartered accountancy training it may well be that a different picture obtains in smaller firms. For example, the suggestion that examinations are viewed negatively (i.e. they are only an issue when a trainee fails) may be less true in environments where pass rates are lower.

Not only was the study confined to Big Six firms, but, within this, to two firms only. We are not in a position to state whether the account we have presented applies in the other Big Six firms. However, we consider it highly likely that it does. The common general background shared by trainees in all the firms and the similarity of the business they are engaged in would make it unlikely that drastically different notions of the professional obtain in the other four firms. If such differences did exist then we would expect trainees to be aware of this through their contact with the other firms during the recruitment process. Nevertheless, it is to be expected that there are some differences of detail between all of the firms.

By the same token, the study only considered a regional office of each of the firms studied, and this too may be a source of limitation. It is possible that other offices of the same firms would have provided a different picture, especially if there were significant differences in the size of office, its client base and the pool from which recruitment occurs. We did gain a certain amount of anecdotal evidence that the London offices of both firms were in certain respects different to the regional office. However, we think it more likely that such differences impact upon organizational issues rather than those of professional identification. For example, if, as some trainees claim, London offices are more competitive and unfriendly it seems that this would make only a minor difference to the issues we have reported here. Given that staff can and do move between offices, it seems highly unlikely that radically different conceptions of the profession operate between these offices.

Finally, the study was limited in that it only looked at trainees. It may be that different conceptions of the professional exist at higher levels within the profession. This limitation was partly imposed by costs consideration but it should be said that there are good analytical reasons to focus on trainees. Precisely because they are trainees they are undergoing the most important passage in their professional formation. Even if they subsequently learn different senses of professional identity it remains the case that this will be against the background of what they have learned as trainees. However, we recognize that, just as we stated earlier that the process of professional socialization has no fixed starting point, so too it has no fixed end point, and certainly not at the end of training.

Summary

This book summarises the findings of a qualitative research project which sought to establish the nature of the professional socialization of trainee chartered accountants working in Big Six firms. The findings were that:

- Professional socialization is conducted largely at the level of the organization.
- Formal and informal socialization processes are not strictly separate.
- Socialization processes include recruitment; appraisal; mentoring; training; socializing and peer groups.
- The trainees' dominant understanding of professional identity is in terms of appropriate behaviour defined in terms of appearance and personal conduct in front of 'clients'.
- Trainees do not typically understand professional identity in terms of the possession of knowledge, nor accreditation to practice nor a public service ethic.
- Trainees' understanding of professional behaviour relates to client service rather than to public service, and they typically understand the client as the management rather than the owners of a company.
- Trainees typically view the Chartered qualification as a passport to general career success in areas associated with 'business' and 'management' rather than as the entry to a career as professional accountants.
- Trainees typically view their examinations as a hurdle to be jumped rather than as having value as the bases of their knowledge and expertise.
- The above findings do not vary significantly between the two firms studied nor between different specialist divisions within the firms.

Bibliography

Abbott, A. (1988), *The System of Professions*, Chicago: Chicago University Press.

Accountancy Age (1996), '£30K Spent Socialising', 14th March, p.35.

Ackroyd, S. (1996), 'The Quality of Qualitative Methods; Qualitative or Quality Methodology for Organization Studies', *Organization*, vol. 3, pp.439-451.

Anderson, F., Grey C. and Robson K. (1996), 'Discursive Fragmentation in the Professional Socialization of Big Six Trainees', Paper presented to the *Critical Perspectives on Accounting Conference*, New York, April.

Atkinson, P. (1981), *The Clinical Experience: The Construction and Reconstruction of Medical Reality*, Farnborough: Gower.

Atkinson, P. (1983), 'The Reproduction of the Professional Community', in R. Dingwall and P. Lewis (eds), *The Sociology of the Professions*, London: Macmillan.

Auerbach, J.S. (1976), *Unequal Justice: Lawyers and Social Change in Modern America,* New York: Oxford University Press.

Becker, H.S. (1952), 'The Nature of a Profession', in National Society for the Study of Education, *Education for the Professions*, Chicago: University of Chicago Press.

Becker, H.S., Geer, B., Hughes, E.C. and Strauss, A.L. (1961), *Boys in White,* Chicago: University of Chicago Press.

Berger, P. and Luckmann, T. (1966), *The Social Construction of Reality*, London: Penguin.

Briloff, A. (1972), *Unaccountable Accounting*, New York: Harper & Row.

Bryman, A. and Burgess, R. (eds), (1994), *Analyzing Qualitative Data*, London: Routledge.

Bucher, R. and Stelling, J.G. (1977), *Becoming Professional*, London and California: Sage.

Bucher, R. and Strauss, A.L. (1961), 'Professions in Process', *American Journal of Sociology*, vol. 66, pp.325-334.

Bunton, R.B. (1985), *Reproducing Psychiatry: An Ethnographic Study on Entry to an Occupation*, PhD Thesis, University of Wales College of Cardiff.

Campbell-Jones, S. (1979), *In Habit: An Anthropological Study of Working Nuns*, London: Falmer.

Carey, J. (1969), *The Rise of the Accountancy Profession from Technical to Professional 1896-1936*, New York: AICPA.

Carey, J. (1970), *The Rise of the Accounting Profession to Responsibility and Authority: 1937-1969*, New York: AICPA.

Carr-Saunders, A.M. and Wilson, P.A. (1934), *The Professions*, Oxford: Oxford University Press.

Cassell, C. and Symon, G. (eds), (1994), *Qualitative Methods in Organizational Research: A Practical Guide*, London: Sage.

Catterall, M. and Maclaren, P. (1996), 'Metamorph 4 for Windows', *Management Learning*, vol. 27, pp.487-490.

Coffey, A.J. (1993), *Double Entry: The Professional and Organizational Socialization of Graduate Accountants*, PhD Thesis, University of Wales College Cardiff.

Coffey, A.J. (1994), '"Timing is Everything"; Graduate Accountants, Time and Commitment', *Sociology*, vol. 28, pp.943-956.

Coffey, A.J., Holbrook, B. and Atkinson, P. (1996), 'Qualitative Data Analysis: Technologies and Representations', *Sociological Research*, vol. 1, http://www.socresonline.org.uk/socresonline/1/1/4.html.

Collins, R. (1975), *Conflict Sociology: Towards an Explanatory Science*, New York: Academic Press.

Collins, R. (1979), *The Credential Society: An Historical Sociology of Education and Stratification*, New York: Academic Press.

Collins, R. (1981), *Sociology Since Midcentury: Essays in Theory Cumulation*, New York: Academic Press.

Cooper, D.J., Puxty, A.G., Robson, K. and Willmott, H. (1996), 'The Regulation of Accounting and Accountants in the UK', *Critical Perspectives on Accounting*, vol. 7, pp.589-613.

Coser, L.A. (1974), *Greedy Institutions: Patterns of Undivided Commitment*, New York: The Free Press.

Cousins, J. and Sikka, P. (1993), 'Accounting for Change - Facilitating Power and Accountability', *Critical Perspectives on Accounting*, March, vol. 4, pp.53-72.

Cousins, J. Mitchell, A. and Sikka, P. (1993), 'Secret Government and Privileged Interests', *Political Quarterly*, July-September, vol. 64, p.306.

Dandridge, T.C. (1986), 'Ceremony as an Integration of Work and Play', *Organization Studies*, vol. 7, pp.159-170.

Davison, I.H. (1987), *The Twilight of the Profession?*, Paper presented to the Conservative Accountants Group, Published by Arthur Andersen, London.

Dean, R.A. (1983), 'Reality Shock: The Link Between Socialisation and Organisational Commitment', *Journal of Management Development*, vol. 2, pp.55-65.

Dean, R.A., Ferris, K.R. and Konstans, L. (1988), 'Occupational Reality Shock and Organizational Commitment: Evidence from the Accounting Profession', *Accounting, Organizations and Society*, vol. 13, pp.235-250.

Denzin, N. and Lincoln, Y. (eds) (1994), *Handbook of Qualitative Research*, Thousand Oaks, CA: Sage.

Derber, C. (ed), (1982), *Professionals as Workers: Mental Labour in Advanced Capitalism*, Boston, MA: G.K. Hall.

Dey, I. (1993), *Qualitative Data Analysis*, London: Routledge.

Dingwall, R. (1976), 'Accomplishing Profession', *Sociological Review*, vol. 24, pp.331-349.

Dingwall, R. (1979), *The Social Organization of Health Visiting*, Beckenham: Croom Helm.

Dingwall, R. and Lewis, P. (eds) (1983), *The Sociology of the Professions*, London: Macmillan.

Dirsmith, M.W., Heian, J.B. and Covaleski, M.A. (1997), 'Structure and Agency in an Institutionalized Setting: The Application and Social Transformation of Control in the Big Six', *Accounting, Organizations and Society*, vol. 22, pp.1-17.

Easterby-Smith, M. and Thorpe, R. (1990), *Doing Management Research*, London: Sage.

Eisenberger, R., Huntington, R., Hutchinson, S. and Sowa, D. (1986), 'Perceived Organizational Support', *Journal of Applied Psychology*, vol. 71, pp.500-507.

Feldman, D.C. (1981), 'The Multiple Socialization of Organization Members', *Academy of Management Review*, vol. 6, pp.309-318.

Fielding, N.G. (1988), *Joining Forces: Police Training, Socialization and Occupational Competence*, London and New York: Routledge.

Fielding, N., and Lee, R. (eds) (1991), *Using Computers in Qualitative Research*, London: Sage.

Freidson, E. (1970), *Professional Dominance: The Social Structure of Medical Care*, New York: Atherton Press.

Freidson, E. (1986), *Professional Powers: A Study of the Institutionalization of Formal Knowledge*, Chicago: University of Chicago Press.

Freidson, E. (1988 [1970b]), *Profession of Medicine: A Study in the Sociology of Applied Knowledge*, Chicago: University of Chicago Press.

Freidson, E. (1994), *Professionalism Reborn; Theory, Prophecy and Policy*, Cambridge: Polity Press.

Giddens, A. (1974), *Positivism and Sociology*, London: Heinemann.

Giddens, A. (1979), *Central Problems in Social Theory: Action, Structure and Contradiction in Social Analysis*, London: Macmillan.

Giddens, A. (1984), *The Constitution of Society*, Cambridge: Polity.

Glaser, B.G. and Strauss, A. (1967), *The Discovery of Grounded Theory*, Chicago: Aldine.

Goffman, E. (1959), *The Presentation of Self in Everyday Life*, Harmondsworth: Penguin.

Goode, W.E. (1957), 'Community Within a Community: The Professions', *American Sociological Review*, pp.194-200.

Greenwood, E. (1957), 'Attributes of a Profession', *Social Work*, pp.44-55.

Grey, C. (1994), 'Career as Project of the Self and Labour Process Discipline', *Sociology*, vol. 28, pp.479-497.

Grey, C. (1998), 'On Being a Professional in a Big Six Firm', *Accounting, Organizations and Society* (in press).

Halfpenny, P. (1982), *Positivism and Sociology: Explaining Social Life*, London: Allen & Unwin.

Hall, R.H. (1983), 'Theoretical Trends in the Sociology of the Professions', *Sociological Quarterly*, vol. 24, pp.5-23.

Halliday, T.C. (1989), 'Legal Professions and Politics: Neocorporatist Variations on the Pluralist Theme of Liberal Democracies', in R.L. Abel and P.S. Lewis (eds), *Lawyers in Society, 3: Comparative Theories*, Berkeley: University of California Press, pp.375-426.

Hammersley, M. and Atkinson, P. (1983), *Ethnography, Principles in Practice*, London: Routledge.

Hanlon, G. (1994), *The Commercialisation of Accountancy; Flexible Accumulation and the Transformation of the Service Class,* Basingstoke: Macmillan.

Hans, J. and Shaffir, W. (1977), 'The Professionalization of Medical Students: Developing Competence and a Cloak of Competence', *Symbolic Interaction,* vol. 1, pp.71-88.

Haring, J.R. (1979), 'Accounting Rules and "the Accounting Establishment"', *Journal of Business,* pp.507-520.

Harper, R.R. (1988), 'The Fate of Idealism in Accountancy', *Second Interdisciplinary Perspectives on Accounting Conference,* University of Manchester, 11-13 July.

Haug, M.R. (1988), 'A Re-Examination of the Hypothesis of Physician Deprofessionalization', *Millbank Quarterly,* vol. 66 (Suppl 2).

Hockey, J. (1986), *Squaddies: Portrait of a Subculture,* Exeter: University of Exeter Press.

Hopwood, A., Page, M. and Turley, W.S. (1989), *The Future of the Profession,* London: ICAEW.

Hopwood, A., Page, M. and Turley, W.S. (1990), *Understanding a Changing Environment,* London: ICAEW/Prentice-Hall.

Horowitz, J.H. (1978), 'Management Control in France, Great Britain and Germany', *Columbia Journal of World Business,* Summer, pp.512-521.

Hughes, E.C. (1958), *Men and their Work,* Glencoe: Free Press.

Hughes, E.C. (1971), *The Sociological Eye,* New York: Aldine.

Hussein, M.C. and Ketz, J.C. (1980), 'Ruling Elites of the FASB: A Study of the "Big Eight"', *Journal of Accounting, Auditing and Finance,* pp.354-367.

ICAEW/MORI (1996), *Survey of Members' Views on Education and Training.*

Jackson, N. and Carter, P. (1995), 'The "Fact" of Management', *Scandinavian Journal of Management,* vol. 11, pp.197-208.

Johnson, T.J. (1972), *Professions and Power,* London and Basingstoke: The Macmillan Press.

Johnson, T.J. (1977), 'The Professions in the Class Structure', in R. Scase (ed), *Industrial Society: Class, Cleavage and Control,* London: George Allen and Unwin.

Johnson, T.J. (1980), 'Work and Power' in G. Esland and G. Salaman (eds), *The Politics of Work and Occupations,* Milton Keynes: Open University Press.

Jones, E. (1981), *Accounting and the British Economy,* London: Batsford.

Kanter, R.M. (1972), *Commitment and Community: Communes and Utopias in Sociological Perspective,* Cambridge Mass: Harvard University Press.

Kelle, U. (ed) (1995), *Computer-Aided Qualitative Data Analysis. Theory, Methods and Practice,* London: Sage.

Larkin, G. (1983), *Occupational Monopoly and Modern Medicine,* London: Tavistock.

Larson, M.S. (1977), *The Rise of Professionalism: A Sociological Analysis,* London: University of California Press.

Latour, B. (1987), *Science in Action,* Milton Keynes: Open University Press.

Lee, R. (1993), *Doing Research on Sensitive Topics,* London: Routledge.

Lee, R. and Fielding, N. (1996), 'Qualitative Data Analysis: Representations of a Technology: A Comment on Coffey, Holbrook and Atkinson', *Sociological Research Online*, vol. 1, http://www.socresonline/socresonline/1/4/if.html.

Legge, K. (1995), *Human Resource Management. Rhetorics and Realities*, Basingstoke: Macmillan.

Littleton, A.C. and Zimmerman, L. (1962), *Accounting Evolution to 1900*, New York: Garland.

Loft, A. (1986), 'Towards a Critical Understanding of Accounting: The Case of Cost Accounting in the UK 1914-25', *Accounting, Organizations and Society*, pp.137-169.

McCloskey, D. (1984), *The Rhetoric of Economics*, London: Macmillan.

Macdonald, K.M. (1984), 'Professional Formation: The Case of Scottish Accountants', *British Journal of Sociology*, vol. 35, pp.174-189.

Macdonald, K.M. (1985), 'Social Closure and Occupational Registration', *Sociology*, vol. 19, pp.541-556.

Macdonald, K.M. (1989), 'Building Respectability', *Sociology*, vol. 23, pp.55-80.

Macdonald, K.M. (1995), *The Sociology of the Professions*, London: Sage.

Melia, K.M. (1987), *Learning and Working: The Occupational Socialization of Nurses*, London: Tavistock.

Merton, R.K., Reader, G. and Kendall, P.L. (eds) (1957), *The Student Physician: Introducing Studies in the Sociology of Medical Education'*, Cambridge, Mass: Harvard University Press.

Miles, M. and Hubermann, A. (eds) (1994), *Qualitative Data Analysis: An Expanded Sourcebook*, London: Sage.

Miller, S.J. (1970), *Prescription for Leadership: Training for the Medical Elite*, Chicago: Aldine.

Millerson, G. (1964), *The Qualifying Associations*, London: Routledge and Kegan Paul.

Mumford, E. (1970), *Interns: From Students to Physicians*, Cambridge, Mass: Harvard University Press.

Murphy, R. (1988), *Social Closure*, Oxford: The Clarendon Press.

Olesen, V. and Whittaker, E.W. (1968), *The Silent Dialogue: The Social Psychology of Professional Socialization*, San Francisco: Jossey Bass.

Olesen, V. and Whittaker, E.W. (1970), 'Critical Notes on Sociological Studies of Professional Socialization', in J.A. Jackson (eds), *Professions and Professionalization*, Cambridge: Cambridge University Press, pp.179-221.

Parkin, F. (1979), *Marxism and Class Theory: A Bourgeois Critique*, London: Tavistock Publications.

Parry, O. (1988), *The Journalism School: The Occupational Socialization of Graduate Journalists*, PhD Thesis, University College, Cardiff.

Parsons, T. (1951), *The Social System*, New York: The Free Press.

Parsons, T. (1954), 'The Professions and Social Structure', in T. Parsons, *Essays in Sociological Theory*, Glencoe, IL: The Free Press.

Parsons, T. (1964), 'Definitions of Health and Illness in the Light of American Values and Social Structure', *Social Structure and Personality*, New York: The Free Press.

Parsons, T. (1968), 'Professions', *International Encyclopaedia of the Social Sciences*, New York.

Peters, T. and Waterman, A. (1982), *In Search of Excellence*, New York: Harper & Row.

Platt, A.M. (1969), *The Child Savers: The Invention of Delinquency*, London: Tavistock.

Power, M.K. (1991), 'Educating Accountants: Towards a Critical Ethnography', *Accounting, Organizations and Society*, vol. 16, pp.333-353.

Richards, T. and Richards, L. (1994), 'Using Computers in Qualitative Research', in N. Denzin and Y. Lincoln (eds), *Handbook of Qualitative Research*, Thousand Oaks, CA: Sage, pp.445-462.

Robson, K., and Cooper, D.J. (1990), 'Understanding the Development of the Accountancy Profession in the UK', in D.J. Cooper and T. Hopper, *Critical Accounts*, London: Macmillan.

Robson, K., Willmott, H., Cooper, D.J. and Puxty, A.G. (1994), 'The Ideology of Professional Regulation and the Markets for Accounting Labour: Three Episodes in the Recent History of the U.K. Accountancy Profession', *Accounting, Organizations and Society*, vol. 19, pp.527-553.

Rothman, D.J. (1971), *The Discovery of the Asylum*, Boston: Little, Brown.

Rueschemeyer, D. (1973), *Power and the Discussion of Labour*, Cambridge: Polity Press.

Rueschemeyer, D. (1986), *Power and the Division of Labour*, Cambridge: Polity Press.

Schon, D. (1987), *The Reflective Practioner*, San Francisco: Jossey-Bass.

Scott, D.R. (1931), *The Cultural Significance of Accounts*, Houston, Texas: Scholars Book Co.

Seidel, J. (1988), *The Ethnograph: A User's Guide*, Littleton, CO: Qualis Research Associates.

Seidel, J., Friese, R. and Leonard, J. (1995), *The Ethnograph: A User's Guide*, Littleton, CO: Qualis Research Associates.

Seron, C. and Ferris, K. (1995), 'Negotiating Professionalism: The Gendered Social Capital of Flexible Time', *Work and Occupations*, vol. 22, pp.22-47.

Sikka, P. and Willmott, H. (1995), 'The Power of "Independence": Defending and Extending the Jurisdiction of Accounting in the United Kingdom', *Accounting, Organizations and Society*, August, vol. 20, pp.547-581.

Silverman, D. (1985), *Qualitative Methodology and Sociology*, Aldershot: Gower.

Silverman, D. (1993), *Interpreting Qualitative Data*, London: Sage.

Simunic, D. (1980), 'The Pricing of Audit Services: Theory and Evidence', *Journal of Accounting Research*, pp.161-190.

Solomons, D. (1978), 'The Politicization of Accounting', *Journal of Accountancy*, pp.65-72.

Solomons, D. (1986), *Making Accounting Policy*, Oxford: Oxford University Press.

Spencer, H. (1914 [1896]), *The Principles of Sociology*, vol. 3, part 7, New York: Appleton.

Stacey, N. (1954), *English Accountancy: A Study in Social and Economic History*, London: Gee & Co.

Stamp, E. and Marley, W. (1970), *Accounting Principles and the City Code: The Case for Reform*, London: Butterworths.

Strauss, A. (1987), *Qualitative Analysis for Social Scientists*, Cambridge: Cambridge University Press.

Tesch, R. (1990), *Qualitative Analysis: Analysis Types and Software Tools*, London: Falmer Press.

Tesch, R. (1991), 'Software for Qualitative Researchers: Analysis Needs and Program Capabilities', in N. Fielding and R. Lee (eds), *Using Computers in Qualitative Research*, London: Sage.

Townley, B. (1994), *Reframing Human Resource Management - Power, Ethics and the Subject at Work*, London: Sage.

Tricker, R.I. (1983), *Governing the Institute*, London: Institute of Chartered Accountants in England and Wales.

Waddington, I. (1984), *The Medical Profession in the Industrial Revolution*, London: Humanities Press.

Wagneschein, M. (1950), *Reality Shock: A Study of Beginning Elementary School Teachers*, Masters Thesis, University of Chicago.

Weaver, A. and Atkinson, P. (1994), *Microcomputing and Qualitative Data Analysis*, London: Avebury, Cardiff Papers in Qualitative Research Series.

Weitzman, E. and Miles, M. (1995), *Computer Programs for Qualitative Data Analysis: A Software Sourcebook*, Newbury Park, CA: Sage.

Wilensky, H.J. (1964), 'The Professionalization of Everyone?', *American Journal of Sociology*, pp.1425-1146.

Willmott, H.C. (1986), 'Organizing the Profession', *Accounting, Organizations and Society*, vol. 11, pp.555-580.

Willmott, H.C., Cooper, D.J, Puxty, A. and Lowe, E.A. (1993), 'Making 'Interests Coincide': An Examination of Discourses of Governance in the ICAEW', *Accounting, Auditing and Accountability Journal*, vol. 6, pp.68-93.

Winch, P. (1958), *The Idea of a Social Science*, London: RKP.

Wood, S. (1989), 'New Wave Management', *Work, Employment and Society*, vol. 3, pp.379-402.

Worsley, F.E. (1985), *Governing the Institute*, London: Institute of Chartered Accountants in England and Wales.

Zaccaro, S.J. and Dobbins, G.H. (1989), 'Contrasting Group and Organizational Commitment: Evidence for Differences Among Multilevel Attachments', *Journal of Organizational Behaviour*, vol. 10, pp.267-273.

Index

Abbott, A. 1, 3, 8, 17, 20-21, 127
accountancy trainees (*see also* clients, examinations, human resource management, gender, physical appearance, social events, time, training)
  appraisal/rating of 55, 60-65, 81-82, 115
  and behaviour 29-34, 55, 60, 65-66, 68-69, 72, 78, 85-91
  and careers 55, 58, 75, 77, 91-94, 121, 131-133
  characteristics 58-60, 102-107, 112-113
  and commitment 31, 77
  competition amongst 76-78
  educational background of 57, 117
  and examinations 81, 91-96, 98-101
  and functional specialisms 44, 46, 98, 108-123
  and hierarchy 43, 45, 73-74
  and ICAEW 71, 95, 100, 110
  instrumentalism of 93, 100, 131-133
  previous research on 2, 29-34, 125
  and qualification 31
  and salaries 61, 105
  and year group 77, 116
accountancy profession (*see also* accountancy trainees, Big Six firms, firms, ICAEW) 4, 8-15
  and public service ethic 8-9
  regulation of 9, 11-12
action-structure dualism 38-39

Atkinson, P. 19, 23-25, 41, 48-49, 53, 85

Becker, H. 3, 23-24, 27-28, 85, 126
'Big Six' firms (*see also* accountancy profession, firms)
  'firm A' 5-6, 42-44, 62, 102-105, 119-120
  'firm B' 5-6, 13, 42, 44-46, 62, 105-107, 119
  and smaller firms 12, 135

clients
  and professional behaviour 21, 29, 30, 55, 59-60, 66-68, 76, 78, 81, 88-89
Coffey, A. 2, 19, 23-25, 28-33, 48-68, 84-85, 87, 126
Computer Aided Qualitative Data Analysis (CAQDAS) (*see also* The Ethnograph) 5, 36, 48
consultancy services 108

Dingwall, R. 1, 18, 20, 28, 60, 126

Ethnograph, The (data analysis package) 5, 48-53
  codes used 51-52
  and interpretation 49, 52-53
  procedures 48-53
examinations (*see also* training) 30, 91-96
  Graduate Conversion Course (GCC) 67, 74, 95, 97
  finals 81, 99
  intermediate 81, 97
  modes of study 67, 118

For Product Safety Concerns and Information please contact our EU
representative GPSR@taylorandfrancis.com Taylor & Francis Verlag GmbH,
Kaufingerstraße 24, 80331 München, Germany

Printed and bound by CPI Group (UK) Ltd, Croydon, CR0 4YY

12/05/2025

01867549-0001